D0563886

"SAILOR, BEWARE!"

A Comedy

PHILIP KING & FALKLAND CARY

French's
Acting
Edition

"SAILOR, BEWARE!"

A Comedy in Three Acts

by

PHILIP KING

and

FALKLAND CARY

SAMUEL FRENCH

FRENCH

LONDON
NEW YORK TORONTO SYDNEY HOLLYWOOD

"SAILOR, BEWARE!"

Produced at the Strand Theatre, London, on the 16th February 1955, with the following cast of characters—

(in the order of their appearance)

Edie Hornett	*Ann Wilton*
Emma Hornett	*Peggy Mount*
Mrs Lack	*Myrette Morven*
Henry Hornett	*Cyril Smith*
Albert Tufnell, A.B.	*Richard Coleman*
Carnoustie Bligh, A.B.	*James Copeland*
Daphne Pink	*Jean Burgess*
Shirley Hornett	*Sheila Shand Gibbs*
The Reverend Oliver Purefoy	*Anthony Marlowe*

Produced by Melville Gillam

Settings by Michael Eve

SYNOPSIS OF SCENES

The action of the play passes in the living-room of the Hornetts' house in a small inland town

ACT I

5.15 p.m. on an afternoon in September

ACT II

Scene 1   9.30 the same evening
Scene 2   10.45 the following morning

ACT III

About an hour later

Time—the present

A*

"SAILOR, BEWARE!"

ACT I

SCENE-—*The living-room of the Hornetts' house in a small inland town. Five-fifteen p.m. on an afternoon in September.*

The door to the hall, front door and staircase is up L, *and a door* R *of the back wall leads to the kitchen and back yard. A window* C *of the back wall overlooks the street. There is a kitchen range* R. *The furnishings are ordinary in taste, but everything about the room is spotless. A settee of the "Put-U-Up" variety stands* LC. *There is a dining-table* C *with chairs* R *and* L *of it. A sideboard stands between the door* R *and the window. There is an armchair above the fireplace and a fireside chair down* R. *A small table stands in the window recess, and another small table down* R *has a radio receiver on it. There are upright chairs up* R, *up* LC *and* L. *There is a wall cabinet on the wall* L *and a mirror on the wall below the fireplace. At night the room is lit by an electric pendant* C, *with its switch below the door* L.

(See the Ground Plan and Photograph of the Scene)

When the CURTAIN *rises, the room is empty. The front-door bell rings off.* EDIE HORNETT *rushes on* R *from the kitchen. She is a thin, nondescript spinster of fortyish. She carries a large pot of tea. She crosses hurriedly towards the door* L, *then realizes she has the teapot in her hand. She "tut-tuts", puts the teapot on the left end of the sideboard and exits* L. *After a moment, she re-enters. She carries a large cardboard box which she deposits on the table* C. *She flutters over it, as if she is about to open it, but does not; she reads the label, then takes a handkerchief from her pocket, sniffs, dabs her eyes, crosses to the door* L *and calls.*

EDIE (*calling*) Emma! It's come.

(EMMA HORNETT *enters* L. *She is a large woman of Edie's age; masterful and sharp tongued*)

EMMA (*as she enters*) What's come?
EDIE. The wedding cake. I'd just made the tea when . . .
EMMA. Where is it?
EDIE. It'll be in the box.
EMMA. The tea.
EDIE. Oh, I'll bring it in. It's all ready.

(EDIE *exits* R. EMMA *crosses to the fireplace, takes a pair of scissors from the mantelpiece, returns to the table* C, *cuts the string of the box and lifts out the cake.*

EDIE *re-enters* R. *She carries a tray with cups etc. for two. She puts the tray on the table* C)

Oh, Emma—isn't it beautiful? (*She weeps*)

1

EMMA. Oh, Lord! Now don't you start. (*She replaces the cake in the box, then puts the box on the settee*)

EDIE. I'm sorry, Emma—I can't help it. It's bringing it all back to me.

EMMA. Good heavens, Edie, that was nearly twenty years ago. Now we won't go into all that if you don't mind. Now let's have a cup of tea and have it quick. There's a lot to be done tonight, yet. (*She looks at the tray*) That's clever, isn't it? Where's the teapot?

EDIE (*fluttering*) Oh, I put it down somewhere, when the bell rang. Now where . . .? Oh, yes. It's on the sideboard. (*She turns to the sideboard*)

EMMA (*alert*) On the . . . (*She darts to the sideboard, snatches up the teapot and looks in horror at the sideboard*) For heaven's sake!

EDIE (*moving to* L *of the sideboard; tremulously*) What is it, Emma?

EMMA (*furiously*) Edie 'Ornett, you haven't the brains you were born with. No more sense than to put a hot teapot down on a polished sideboard. Just look at that big white ring. We'll never get it out.

EDIE. Well, you see, the bell rang . . .

EMMA. A wedding present from my mother, this was, and never so much as a scratch on it all these years, and you have to go and . . .

EDIE. Emma, I'll try and get it out afterwards.

EMMA. *Afterwards!* You'll try and get it out *now*. Go on! Get the furniture polish. Hurry.

(EDIE *scuttles off* R. EMMA *moans over the mark a little longer, then pours herself a cup of tea.*

EDIE *re-enters* R. *She carries a tin of furniture polish and a duster. The duster drops to the floor as she enters*)

EDIE (*as she enters; hopefully*) Here we are, Emma. (*She moves to* R *of Emma and hands her the tin*)

EMMA (*with great exasperation*) "Here we are, Emma!" And what do we put it on with? Our knickers?

EDIE. Oh! (*She looks round for the duster*)

(EMMA *silently appeals to heaven to give her patience, then drinks her tea*)

(*She picks up the duster*) Here we are, Emma.

EMMA (*snatching the duster and moving to the sideboard*) You'll have to put some elbow grease into it. (*She puts some polish on the surface of the sideboard and rubs it in with a circular movement*)

EDIE (*pouring a cup of tea for herself*) Yes, Emma. I'll just pour myself a cup of tea, first.

EMMA. Come and watch.

(EDIE *picks up her cup without the saucer and crosses to* R *of Emma*)

This is how you do it. Rub it round and round till it gets real hot
and keep on rubbing, and it *might* bring it out.

EDIE (*eagerly*) Yes, Emma. (*She puts her cup on the sideboard,
preparatory to taking the duster*)

EMMA (*with a wail of anguish*) For goodness' sake! (*She snatches
Edie's cup from the sideboard*)

EDIE. What . . .?

EMMA. You'll have another mark in a minute. (*She inspects the
sideboard where the cup was, but apparently there is no mark*) I dunno!
You're always moaning 'cos you never got married, but God
knows what sort of a home you'd 'ave 'ad if you 'ad. (*She hands
the cup of tea to Edie*) Here! Get this down you, then get started.
It'll take hours.

(EDIE *almost pours the tea straight down her throat, chokes a little,
hands her cup to Emma, then begins the polishing process*)

(*She puts Edie's cup on the tray, then pours another cup of tea for herself*)
What's the time? (*She moves* RC *and looks at the clock on the mantelpiece*) I'll never get everything done by the time they start
arriving. Daphne's due at any minute, now. Lord, I wish tomorrow was over. (*She sits on the chair* R *of the table* C)

EDIE (*panting as she rubs*) So do I.

EMMA (*sharply*) I don't see what you're worrying about. It
isn't your daughter that's getting married—(*in the same breath*) is
it coming off?

EDIE. No.

EMMA. I know. It won't. Go on, carry on.

EDIE (*moving to* L *of the table* C) It's the thought of seeing
Shirley in her bridal dress. I know I won't be able to bear up.
It'll bring it all back to me.

(MRS LACK'S *voice is heard off* R)

MRS LACK (*off; calling*) Anyone at home?

EMMA (*muttering*) Oh, my . . .

(MRS LACK *appears in the doorway* R. *Much the same age as
Emma, she takes life easily, and other folk's troubles with considerable
pleasure*)

MRS LACK (*as she appears*) It's only me. (*She crosses and stands
up* R *of the settee*)

EDIE (*moving to the sideboard*) It's only Mrs Lack, Emma. (*She
polishes*)

MRS LACK. That's right. It's only me. I don't want to disturb
you, 'cos I know you're busy; but I just thought I'd . . . My!
Look at Edie! She isn't half going it, is she? Gettin' all polished
up for tomorrow, eh, Edie? The great day, eh? (*She looks at the tea
tray*) Oh, you just having a cuppa? I wouldn't have disturbed you
if I'd known, but I thought I'd just . . .

EMMA (*rising; not too sweetly*) You'd better have a cup since you're here. (*She collects the teapot*) I'll have to put some water in.

(EMMA *exits* R)

MRS LACK (*moving above the table, following Emma*) No, don't bother, Emma. I didn't really come in for that—but I thought I'd just . . .

(*But* EMMA *has gone*)

(*She moves to* L *of Edie, then, with a quick look towards the door* R, *she speaks in a quiet voice*) Got you at it, 'asn't she, Edie? She'd drive me up the wall with her everlasting cleaning and polishing.

EDIE (*she is no traitress*) Well, you see . . .

MRS LACK (*picking up the tin of polish*) What does she use? (*She looks at the tin*) "Polisho." Muck!

EDIE. But . . .

MRS LACK (*replacing the tin*) Muck, Edie; that's what it is. I wouldn't use it on the cat. Still, everyone to their taste. You know, you'll 'ave yourself worn out if you go on like that. You'll not be in a fit state for the wedding tomorrow. She oughtn't to make you work like that.

EDIE. Oh, but I'm not going to the wedding, Mrs Lack.

MRS LACK. Not going?

(EDIE *stops polishing*)

EDIE (*with a whimper*) No, I'm not going.

MRS LACK (*aghast*) Your own brother's daughter's wedding, and you're not going. (*With a jerk of her head towards the door* R) Here, does *she* say you can't?

(EDIE *resumes polishing*)

EDIE. No, no, I couldn't bring myself to go. It would bring back too many memories.

MRS LACK (*with great understanding*) Ah, I see what you mean. You mean your Great Sorrow.

EDIE (*nodding vigorously as she rubs*) Ummps!

MRS LACK. Yes, of course, it's only natural you shouldn't want to go. I mean it would be more than flesh and blood could stand, wouldn't it?

EDIE. Ummps!

MRS LACK (*cheerfully*) Yes, of course it would. Watching Shirley standing at the altar rails, and remembering the day when you yourself . . .

EDIE (*now completely abandoned to grief*) Don't. Don't, Mrs Lack. I mustn't think of it. (*She polishes*)

MRS LACK. Of course you mustn't. (*Her voice throbs with inspiration*) "Oh, memories that bless and burn . . ."

EDIE (*almost inspired*) "Oh, barren gain and bitter loss!" (*She rubs briskly*)

(MRS LACK *very practically points to the other end of the sideboard*)

MRS LACK. I should come over a bit if I were you, Edie, or you'll wear an 'ole in it.

(EMMA *enters* R. *She carries the teapot and a cup and saucer*)

EMMA (*it might be an accusation or a statement*) Now, then . . .

MRS LACK (*moving to* L *of the table* C) Ah! It's very kind of you, Emma. I didn't mean to—but I just 'appened to look over the wall—and I saw the door open; so I thought I'd just . . .

EMMA. Sugar?

MRS LACK. Two. (*She sits* L *of the table* C *and giggles*) Well—I'm all ready for the bridegroom.

EMMA. What! (*She pours a cup of tea for Mrs Lack*)

MRS LACK. I mean, I've got the bedroom ready for him and his best man. I hope they'll be comfortable.

(EMMA *hands the cup of tea to Mrs Lack, then sits* R *of the table* C)

I'm not used to . . . But when you asked me if I could put them up for tonight—well, it was only neighbourly, wasn't it? (*She sips her tea*)

EMMA. Tea all right?

MRS LACK. Yes, thanks. (*With purpose*) Mind you, it would have been expensive for them if they'd had to go round to the *Rose and Crown*, wouldn't it?

(EDIE *polishes half-heartedly*)

EMMA (*rather shortly*) I shall see to it that you're paid for your inconvenience.

MRS LACK. Do you want me to give them breakfast?

EMMA. You'll 'ave to, won't you? That's the whole point of 'em coming to you.

MRS LACK. What? To get a good breakfast?

EMMA (*very shortly*) To keep them out of the way so the bridegroom doesn't see the bride before the wedding.

(EDIE *stops polishing and moves above the table* C)

EDIE. Albert mustn't see Shirley before the wedding whatever 'appens. That'd be unlucky. (*She moves to the sideboard and resumes polishing*)

EMMA (*waving Edie's remark away*) Never you mind about who sees who—when or where. Is it coming off?

EDIE (*forcing herself to be truthful*) Not so you'd notice.

EMMA. Well, rub harder.

EDIE. Yes, Emma. (*She rubs more vigorously*)

MRS LACK. Well, I hope they'll be comfortable at my place. I'll do my best for them, I'm sure.

Emma. I shouldn't worry yourself. They're both sailors, so they should be used to roughing it.

(Mrs Lack *does not know how to take this and gives Emma a look. Edie polishes half-heartedly*)

It isn't *their* comfort tonight—it's Shirley's happiness in the future that I'm concerned about.

Mrs Lack. Yes. It must be a worry when your only daughter takes the plunge—wondering if she's going in at the right end—so to speak—a worry for you and your husband.

Emma (*with fine scorn*) Him! A lot he worries. All he thinks about is his blessed ferrets. (*She blows her nose*)

Mrs Lack (*gaily*) Oh, yes. Mr 'Ornett and his ferrets. He does think a lot of them, doesn't he?

Emma. He thinks about 'em so much he should've married one. Nasty stinking things. They'd be out of the back yard this minute if I had my way.

Edie (*moving above the table* c) Oh, Emma, you wouldn't take Henry's ferrets away from him, would you? Why, it'd break his heart. Always been fond of dumb creatures, he has. I remember when he was a little boy he 'ad an 'edge'og—and he gave it all his love . . .

Emma. Well, he has a daughter, now, and he should give her a bit of his love. Never mind about ferrets and 'edge'ogs. (*She jerks her head towards the sideboard*)

(Edie *resumes polishing*)

Not one scrap of interest has he taken in Shirley's wedding, he hasn't. Left it all to me. But this I will say, and I don't care who hears me say it—are you listening, Edie—if Shirley's marriage turns out wrong, to my dying day I'll say that 'Enry's to blame.

Mrs Lack. What makes you say that?

Emma. It was 'Enry first brought this Albert Tufnell to the house, or our Shirley'd never have met him.

Edie (*moving above the table* c) It was love at first sight.

Emma (*glaring at Edie*) Get on.

(Edie *resumes polishing*)

Mrs Lack. Well, what about his people?

Emma. Yes, what about them? That's what I'd like to know. He hasn't got any. He was brought up in a Sailors' Orphanage—he *says*.

Mrs Lack (*relishing this*) H'mm! Fishy, isn't it? Well, I'm sure I *hope* it turns out all right. It might. You never know.

Emma. Heaven knows I've tried to talk to Shirley. I've tried to stop her doing something she might regret for the rest of her life. The times I've said to her, "Shirley, you know what sailors are."

Mrs Lack (*joyfully*) Yes, aren't they?

EMMA. But I might as well talk to myself for what notice she takes.

EDIE (*stopping polishing*) They love each other, Emma.

(EMMA *looks at* EDIE *who hastily resumes polishing*)

MRS LACK. You can't set much store by that, Edie girl, can you, Emma?

EMMA. I say, and I've always said, it's the uniform that Shirley's fallen for. She'll change her tune when she sees him without it.

MRS LACK (*with rather a naughty giggle*) Well, of course, that all depends . . .

EMMA. He won't look so la-di-da in a suit of dungarees.

MRS LACK (*soberly*) Oh? I see what you mean.

EMMA. He's only got another three months to do in the Navy; then he'll have to settle down and do a proper job of work.

(*The front door is heard to slam off* L)

(*In the same breath; calling*) That you, Henry?

HENRY (*off* L; *calling dolefully*) Yes.

EMMA (*calling*) You wiped your feet?

HENRY (*off*) Yes.

EMMA (*rising and moving above the table* C) That passage is all polished up for tomorrow. I don't want you . . .

(HENRY HORNETT *enters* L. *He is a smallish man of fifty. He wears a shapeless, but clean, blue suit*)

(*She looks and speaks disparagingly at Henry*) Oh. I suppose you'll want a cup of tea?

MRS LACK. Hello, Mr Hornett.

HENRY (*grunting*) Hello. (*To Emma*) Cup of . . .! I want more than a cup of tea. (*He crosses to the fireplace, takes his pipe and tobacco pouch from his pocket and puts them on the mantelpiece*) I want my tea proper. (*He removes his jacket and puts it on the back of the armchair*)

EMMA (*sharply*) Now, don't you start! I told you before you went out this morning nobody's having their teas till seven o'clock. Do you want a cup of tea now, or don't you?

HENRY (*removing his tie and stiff collar*) I'm not fussy.

EMMA. Well, I'm not going down on my knees to ask you.

HENRY. If there's any left in the pot, I'll *have* it. If there isn't, it doesn't matter. Edie, have you fed the ferrets?

(EMMA *pours a cup of tea for Henry in her own cup*)

EDIE (*moving above the armchair*) At dinner time, I did, Henry.

EMMA. Never mind about . . .

HENRY (*to Edie; interrupting*) Did Rosie take her dinner? How's she looking? Nothing happened yet?

A**

(EDIE *moves to the sideboard and polishes*)

EDIE (*very vaguely*) Ooh, I didn't stop to look, Henry. I was late. I had to get back to work.

HENRY. I'd better go and see.

EMMA. And what about your cup of tea?

HENRY (*putting his tie and collar on the back of the armchair*) If you'd pour it out instead of talking about it so much . . . (*He moves towards the door* R)

EMMA (*picking up the cup of tea and crossing to* L *of Henry*) And if you'd give your mind to things that really mattered instead of . . . (*She hands the tea to Henry*)

(HENRY *swallows the tea in one gulp and makes a wry face immediately afterwards*)

Ferrets! I should have thought you could have given us a rest from them for once. (*She takes the cup from Henry*) Shirley's wedding-day tomorrow and all. (*She moves and puts the cup on the tray*)

HENRY. It's her weddin'—not mine.

EMMA (*flaring*) Well, she's *your* daughter, isn't she?

HENRY. So *you* say.

(HENRY *exits* R)

EMMA (*stunned*) Well, I . . .! (*She moves to the fireplace*)

MRS LACK (*rising with great "to-do"*) Oh, my goodness! Look at the time. I must be getting back. I've got Rita in bed.

EDIE. Oh. Is Rita poorly?

MRS LACK (*moving to the door* L) Oh, it's nothing. Came home from school at dinner time with a headache; so I put her to bed. I think it's just excitement—being one of Shirley's bridesmaids. But I'd better be getting back and see how she is.

(EDIE *polishes*)

Well, I'll expect the boys sometime, then, Emma.

EMMA (*moving above the table* C) You can expect 'em at ten o'clock. They're not stopping here all hours. Shirley will want some rest tonight, and I'll see she gets it.

MRS LACK. Yes, poor thing. (*She giggles*) She won't get much tomorrow, will she?

(EMMA *moves towards the door* R.
HENRY *dashes on* R, *almost colliding with* EMMA)

HENRY (*pushing Emma aside*) Heigh-up! (*To Edie. Excitedly*) Edie! Edie! (*He moves to* R *of Edie*) Edie, warm me a drop of milk, quick, will you. It's happened. Rosie's 'ad 'em. Six of 'em!

EDIE. Six? Six eggs?

HENRY. Eg——! It's time somebody told you the facts of life. (*He pushes past Emma to the door* R) Heigh-up!

(HENRY *dashes off* R)

EDIE. I'd better do it, hadn't I, Emma?

EMMA. Well, I'm not going to, and that's a fact. Go on if you're going.

(EDIE *crosses and exits hurriedly* R, *taking the polish and duster with her*)

(*She moves to the door* R *and calls*) And don't use this morning's milk. There's some that's just on the turn at the back of the shelf.

EDIE (*off; calling*) Yes, Emma.

MRS LACK (*moving up* C *and looking off after Edie*) I expect you find *her* a bit of a handful, don't you?

EMMA (*crossing to the tray*) She's enough to drive me out of my mind. (*She stacks the tea things on the tray*) Always 'arping on about her Great Sorrow.

MRS LACK. Yes, she does 'arp, doesn't she? (*She goes towards the door* L, *then stops*) Oh, no. I mustn't go that way, must I? Paddling on your polished lino. (*She turns and moves towards the door* R, *and pauses beside the sideboard*) Oh, dear! Nasty mark you've got on your sideboard. (*She continues to the door* R) Well, I'll leave you to cope, and thanks for the cup of tea. I didn't really come in for that, you know. (*As she goes*) I 'appened to look over the wall, and saw the door open, so I thought I'd just . . .

(MRS LACK *exits* R. EMMA *gives an exasperated glance towards the door* R)

(*Off*) 'Bye, Edie.

EDIE (*off*) 'Bye, Mrs Lack.

EMMA (*picking up the tray and moving to the door* R) Lord, how that woman 'arps!

(EMMA *exits* R)

(*Off*) Now, what are you doing, Edie?

EDIE (*off*) It's all right, Emma. It's just boiled over. I'll wipe it up.

EMMA (*off*) Edie Hornett—for Heaven's sake!

(*There is a loud knocking on the front door off* L, "*Pom-diddle-om-pom—pom-pom*")

(*Off*) Now, who can that be?

EDIE (*off*) I'll go, Emma.

(EDIE *enters* R, *and crosses to* C. *She carries a small pan of steaming milk*)

EMMA (*off*) Be careful what you're doing with that pan, now, Edie.

(ALBERT'S *voice, almost a roar, is heard off* L)

ALBERT (*off*)   Hello, there.
EDIE (*ecstatically*)   It's Albert! (*She runs to the door* R) Emma, it's Albert!

(ALBERT TUFNELL, A.B., *bursts in* L. *He is aged twenty-three, is good-looking and brimming over with good health and good spirits. He is self-possessed, but not aggressively so. In short, Albert is the ideal sailor girls dream about. He is wearing his A.B. uniform and carries his kitbag over one shoulder and a large suitcase in his left hand*)

ALBERT (*as he enters*)   Anyone at home? (*He kicks the door shut and sees Edie. With a whoop*) Well, if it isn't Jane Russell herself.
EDIE (*bubbling with a girlish giggle*)   Oh, Albert!

(ALBERT *flings his kitbag in the corner up* L *and his suitcase behind the settee*)

ALBERT.   Clear decks for action! (*He holds out his arms to Edie*) Come on! Into my arms!
EDIE (*writhing with delight*)   Oh, Albert! Albert Tufnell! (*She holds the pan of milk at arm's length and backs coyly from him*)
ALBERT.   Are you coming, or do I have to fetch you? (*He moves towards Edie*)
EDIE (*squeaking*)   Albert! Albert, stoppit, do! Mind this pan. It's hot.
ALBERT (*rubbing his hands together*)   So am I. I haven't kissed a woman for three months. (*He snatches the pan from Edie and puts it on the sideboard*) Aunt Edie, you're for it. (*He grabs Edie to him and plants a smacking kiss on both her cheeks*)
EDIE (*a faint voice from another world*)   Oh, Albert!

(ALBERT *whirls Edie round, swings her down* R, *then picks her up in his arms*)

ALBERT.   Aunt Edie, where's the bedroom? (*He carries her down* L)

(EMMA *enters* R *and does not like what she sees*)

EDIE (*kicking her legs and squeaking in a frenzy of not too outraged modesty*)   Ooh, Albert Tufnell, aren't you awful! Put me down. Do you hear? Put me down this minute. Al-bert! Give over. I'm going dizzy.
ALBERT.   Going? I've gone. (*With Edie still in his arms, he is about to sink on to the settee on which stands the box containing the wedding cake*)

(EMMA, *with a scream of anguish, manages to snatch the box away as* ALBERT *sits on the settee*)

EMMA (*clutching the box to her bosom*)   My God! (*She moves to* L *of the armchair*)

(ALBERT, *blissfully unaware of the near calamity, twirls* EDIE *off his knee and rises*)

ALBERT. Ma! (*He crosses to Emma*) If it isn't my dear old ma.

EMMA (*letting out another scream*) Keep away. Edie! Edie! Take this. (*She holds out the box*) Take it while it's safe.

(EDIE *crosses, takes the box from Emma and moves down* L)

ALBERT (*embracing Emma*) That's better! Now we can get to grips.

EMMA (*disentangling herself*) Now stop this. I don't hold with a lot of . . . D'you realize what you nearly did just now?

ALBERT (*cheerfully*) No. What did I do?

EMMA. All your foolin' and larking about. You nearly sat on your wedding cake, nearly flattened it out.

ALBERT. Blimey! Might have made it go round a bit further. Well, how are you, Ma?

EMMA. I'll feel better when you've got yourself sat down and out of harm's way.

(ALBERT *removes his cap, goes up* L, *puts it on the shelf, then picks up his kitbag and leans it against the back of the settee*)

(*She crosses to* LC) Edie, don't stand there holding that in your arms till it melts. Put it down—and somewhere *he* can't get at it.

(EDIE *puts the box on the floor down* L)

Weren't you supposed to be hotting up some milk for Henry?

(EDIE *remembers the pan on the sideboard and looks towards it*)

EDIE. Oooh! (*She runs towards the sideboard*)

(EMMA *moves quickly to the sideboard, gets there first, picks up the pan and examines the sideboard*)

EMMA (*hardly able to speak*) You . . .! Edie 'Ornett, I could kill you.

EDIE. It was an accident, Emma. Albert just came in, and . . .

(ALBERT *is about to open his kitbag*)

EMMA (*fuming*) Never mind about Albert. You did this on purpose. You did it for spite.

ALBERT (*moving to* L *of the sideboard*) Hullo-ullo-ullo!

EMMA (*turning on Albert*) And what are you "Hullo-ullo-ulloing" about?

ALBERT (*cheerfully*) Sounds like a bit of a squall blowing up. Something come adrift, Ma?

EDIE. It's nothing, Albert.

EMMA (*very incensed*) Nothing! No, of course, it's nothing to *you*. It's not your sideboard that's ruined, is it?

(CARNOUSTIE BLIGH, A.B., *unnoticed by the others, peers round the door* L. *He is about the same age as Albert, has his manly beauty, but it inclines to the severe. He takes life seriously, but is extremely popular with his mates, and, to his embarrassment, women are apt to fall for him. His Scotch nationality is not for one moment in doubt once he opens his mouth. He, too, is in sailor's uniform and is wearing his cap*)

No more sense than to put a hot pan . . .

EDIE. But, Emma, I swear I didn't do it on purpose.

ALBERT. 'Course she didn't, Ma. As a matter of fact, I did it. (*He moves between Emma and Edie*) And what have I done?

EMMA. So it was you, was it?

(CARNOUSTIE *takes in the situation, withdraws his head and hastily closes the door*)

Well, just look what you've done. Look! Burnt a big white mark on my sideboard.

| ALBERT (*looking at the mark*) H'mmm! Never mind, Ma. Look —(*he points to the previous mark*) it matches up with that one.

EMMA. Ooooh!

(HENRY *enters* R)

HENRY (*as he enters*) Edie, Edie, Edie. (*He moves to* R *of the table* C) Where's that milk I . . .? (*He sees Albert*) Albert! (*He rushes to Albert and greets him warmly*) When did you get here?

ALBERT (*pleased to see Henry*) How are we, Pop? (*He shakes hands with Henry*)

HENRY. You might have let me know he'd come, Emma.

EMMA (*crossing to the door* R; *muttering*) Bad news travels fast enough.

(EMMA *exits* R)

HENRY (*coughing to cover his embarrassment*) Well, Albert! It's good to see you, boy. Sit you down.

(ALBERT *crosses and sits on the chair down* R)

My, you don't half look well. Plenty of sea breezes, eh? (*He sits in the armchair*)

ALBERT (*with a look towards the door* R) You seem to get a few breezes here, one way and another.

HENRY (*coughing*) H'mm! I wish I'd known you were here. What train did you get? Er—Edie—have we—got a drop of . . .?

(EMMA *enters* R *and moves to the sideboard. She carries the tin of polish and the duster*)

EMMA (*as she enters*) No, we haven't.

EDIE (*fluttering*) Let me do that, Emma.

EMMA. You've done enough damage. Just stay out of my way. That's all I ask. (*She rubs vigorously at the mark on the sideboard*)

HENRY. But, Albert, have you come alone? I thought you were bringing your best man with you.

ALBERT. Good Lord! Carnoustie!

HENRY (*blinking*) Who?

ALBERT. Carnoustie! I'd forgotten all about him. (*He rises*)

HENRY (*rising*) "Car——"! I can't say it. Is that his name?

ALBERT. That's right, Pop. Carnoustie Bligh.

HENRY. Oh, a Russian?

EMMA (*moving to R of the table*) We're having no foreigners in this house. Where is he?

ALBERT (*jerking a finger towards the door* L) He's in the hall, Ma.

EMMA (*moving above the table* C) Paddling about on my polished lino. Albert Tufnell . . .

(ALBERT *crosses below the table* C *to the door* L *and opens it*)

ALBERT (*calling in a very bad Scots accent*) Carnoustie, you Highland hopscotch, show yourself, will you. (*He stands by the doorway "playing" bagpipes and imitating their wails to the tune of "The Road to the Isles"*)

(CARNOUSTIE, *after a short pause, enters* L. *He carries a kitbag and a suitcase*)

I want you to meet the one and only Carnoustie. The braw'est Scot this side of the border.

CARNOUSTIE. Ah'm very pleased indeed to meet ye a'.

EMMA. How do you do, Mr Carnoustie?

CARNOUSTIE (*carefully*) No' *Misterr* Carrrnoustie. Carrrnoustie is ma Chrrristian name.

HENRY. What! Bit funny, isn't it?

(EMMA *moves to the sideboard and polishes*)

CARNOUSTIE. I fail to obsairve any humourr in it, ma'sel'.

ALBERT (*to Henry*) Take it easy, Pop. He's a bit touchy on the old name, you know.

CARNOUSTIE (*patiently explaining*) If it is your wish to address me in forrrmal fashion, ma name wad be Mr Carnoustie Bligh. (*Graciously*) But I'd be honourred if you'd just ca' me Carrrnoustie for shorrrt.

HENRY. Well, well, well! Come on in. Put your things down. Have you been waiting all this time in the hall?

(CARNOUSTIE *puts his kitbag and case behind the settee*)

CARNOUSTIE. Ay.

EMMA (*turning*) Why didn't you come in?

CARNOUSTIE. Because I wasna' askit.

EMMA. That's *your* fault, Albert.

ALBERT. That's all right, Ma, he'll forgive me.

(CARNOUSTIE *removes his cap*)

Now, Carnoustie, that's Pop.

HENRY. How do.

CARNOUSTIE. How do you do, sir?

ALBERT. And Ma.

CARNOUSTIE (*shaking hands with Emma*) How do you do?

EMMA. How do you do? (*She resumes polishing*)

ALBERT (*pushing Edie forward*) And here's Aunt Edie for you, the pride of the harem.

(EDIE *moves to* R *of Carnoustie*)

CARNOUSTIE. I'm happy to meet you, Aunt Edie.

EDIE (*shaking hands*) How do you do?

HENRY. Now, Car—er—Car——

CARNOUSTIE. —noustie.

HENRY (*crossing and sitting* L *of the table* C) That's right. Sit you doon—(*quickly*) down.

(CARNOUSTIE *moves below the settee*)

Er—I expect you could do with a cup of tea.

CARNOUSTIE (*emphatically*) I cuid that!

EMMA. It isn't ready yet.

CARNOUSTIE (*facing facts*) In that case, I'll wait. (*He puts his cap on the left end of the settee*)

ALBERT (*sitting on the right arm of the settee*) Sit down, Carnoustie boy.

(CARNOUSTIE *sits awkwardly on the settee*)

EDIE. Shall I be laying for tea, Emma?

EMMA. You can lay; but no-one's having their tea until seven o'clock. (*To Henry*) I've told you that already once tonight. (*To Edie*) Go on, then—lay.

(EDIE *crosses and exits* R, *leaving the door open*)

HENRY. Now tell me, Car—— Are you interested in ferrets?

CARNOUSTIE. In wha'?

EMMA (*moving above the table* C) Henry!

HENRY. Yes, Emma?

EMMA. Cardustie isn't interested in your ferrets. (*She resumes polishing*)

HENRY (*rising*) Well, I must go and see to Rosie. Make yourself at home.

(HENRY *exits* R, *leaving the door open*)

ALBERT (*rising and moving to* L *of Emma*) Well, Ma, how's my girl? How's the future Mrs Albert Tufnell? (*He takes Emma by the arm*)

    (EMMA *disengages herself, puts down the polish and duster, moves to the table* c *and transfers the scissors to the sideboard*)

EMMA. Yes. I was beginning to wonder when you were going to condescend to ask after her. She's at the hairdressers. (*She gets a crumb-tray and brush from the sideboard*) She should be here any minute. Then she was going down to the station to meet you and —(*with a jerk of her head towards Carnoustie*) him. You weren't supposed to arrive until half-past six. (*She brushes the crumbs from the table* c)

ALBERT (L *of Emma above the table*) We got ashore earlier than we expected, and there was a train just leaving; so we . . . How is she, Ma? Does she love me as much as she used to?

EMMA (*busy with the crumb-tray; shortly*) She loves you as much as she's ever likely to.

ALBERT. Is she looking forward to tomorrow? (*He rubs his hands and winks at Carnoustie*) I know *I* am.

EMMA (*seeing the wink; sharply*) Now then! That's enough of that.

ALBERT (*sobering up*) Ahem! Gone to the hairdressers, has she?

CARNOUSTIE (*flatly*) Can she no' do her own hair? Ma sisterr never goes near the hairdressers.

ALBERT. Carnoustie, you're not in Auchertermochaty now——

    (EMMA *moves to the fireplace and puts the crumbs in the fire*)

—where the bonnie wee lassies put their hair up in thistle stalks. Come on! Let's see about getting our bags unpacked. (*He moves towards his kitbag*)

EMMA. You needn't bother yourselves. You're not stopping here. (*She moves to the sideboard and puts the brush and crumb-tray on it*)

ALBERT. Not? Then where . . .?

EMMA (*taking a cloth from the sideboard drawer*) I've had to make other arrangements—you're both to go next door to Mrs Lack's. (*She moves to the table* c *and spreads the cloth on it*)

ALBERT. Oh? What's the idea, Ma?

EMMA. I haven't room for you for one thing. There's others coming to the wedding besides yourself, you know. We're putting Daphne up.

ALBERT. Daphne?

EMMA. Daphne Pink, my sister's daughter. She's going to be Shirley's chief bridesmaid. I would have thought Shirley'd have told you about her.

ALBERT. Oh, yes, of course she's told me. (*He moves to* L *of Emma*) Here, Ma, she's a bit of all right, isn't she?

EMMA (*heavily*) She's my sister's daughter, if that's what you mean.

ALBERT (*moving above the settee*) No, I didn't.

EMMA. And another reason why you're not staying here. I don't want you in the way tomorrow morning. And don't you get trying to see Shirley, either.

ALBERT. Not see her? (*He takes a step towards Emma*) Not see my future wife?

EMMA. Not in the morning, you won't. Not till she joins you in church. They say it's unlucky for the bride to see the bridegroom before the wedding—(*she moves to the sideboard and picks up the polish and duster*) and heaven knows things look black enough as it is without asking for trouble.

(EMMA *exits* R. ALBERT *stands gazing after her, scratching his head, puzzled. He moves down* R *of the table* C, *crosses to Carnoustie, pats him on the shoulder, then sits* R *of him on the settee*)

ALBERT. Carnoustie—boy.

CARNOUSTIE. Ay?

ALBERT. *Have* I asked for trouble?

CARNOUSTIE. Ay.

ALBERT (*indignantly*) Just because I wanted to see my Shirl.

CARNOUSTIE. No.

ALBERT. What do you mean?

CARNOUSTIE. I dinna mean that ye were speerin' for trouble in tha' way. But in anitherrr.

ALBERT. What itherrr?

CARNOUSTIE. Yon gruesome! Your ma-in-law.

ALBERT. But I'm not marrying her, am I?

CARNOUSTIE. If ye had been, I'd strangle ye wi' ma ain hands. It'd be counted a maircy-killing. Yer fiancée must be exceptional to compensate for—(*with a jerk of his head*) yon.

ALBERT (*brightening a little*) Oh, you'll fall for Shirl all right.

(*The front-door bell rings off*)

(*He rises, moves to the door* R *and calls*) Ma, there's someone at the front door. Shall I go?

(EMMA *enters* R)

EMMA (*as she enters*) You stay where you are. (*She crosses to the door* L) I'll go. I don't want your big feet paddling all over my polished lino. (*She looks at the kitbags*) You can be putting them —them bolsters of yours tidy.

(EMMA *exits* L)

CARNOUSTIE (*in deep disgust*) "Bolsterrs"! (*He rises and moves above the settee*)

(ALBERT *puts his kitbag and case in the window alcove at the left end.* CARNOUSTIE *puts his kitbag and case in the window alcove at the right end*)

DAPHNE (*off*) Aunt Emma. How are you?
EMMA (*off*) I'm very well, thank you, and how's yourself?
DAPHNE (*off*) I thought I was never going to get here. And
how's Shirley? Isn't it all wildly exciting? Oh, have you got half
a crown?

(ALBERT *peeps through the door* L)

EMMA (*off*) No, I have not.

(EMMA's *and* DAPHNE's *voices continue off.* ALBERT *peeps again,
closes the door, then turns to Carnoustie and gives a wolf-whistle*)

ALBERT. Boy! What a peach! You're the best man—so she's
yours—all yours.
CARNOUSTIE (*very gravely*) Now just a minute—Albert, I under-
took to be your best man on one condition—there was to be no
putting me into poseetions of embarrassment wi' young wimmin.
Ye ken tha' I ha'e no time for them, and conseeder as a class
they are . . . (*His voice trails away*)

(DAPHNE PINK *enters* L. *She is a smart, streamlined and salesman-
like piece of goods, with a charming manner and an attractive smile. She
carries a small suitcase.* CARNOUSTIE, *with praiseworthy caution, re-
treats a little, but* ALBERT *dashes to the head of the line*)

DAPHNE (*breaking off from speaking to Emma*) Oh! I didn't know
the Fleet was in. I'm Daphne—Daphne Pink. Now, which is
which?
ALBERT. I'm Albert. The bridegroom. You know, the human
sacrifice. (*He takes Daphne in his arms and kisses her*)

(EMMA *enters* L *and watches disapprovingly.* CARNOUSTIE *stares
open-mouthed at Daphne*)

DAPHNE. You don't waste much time, do you, Albert?
ALBERT. If you think *I'm* fast . . . Meet the hare—(*he gestures to
Carnoustie*) Carnoustie.

(DAPHNE *now "notices" Carnoustie for the first time and likes very
much what she sees. She hands her case to* EMMA, *who puts it behind
the settee*)

DAPHNE (*crossing to Carnoustie*) Oooh! (*She shakes hands*) How
do you do?
CARNOUSTIE (*with difficulty*) Verra—weel.

(DAPHNE *takes a step towards Carnoustie, hopefully expecting the
same treatment as she has received from Albert, but* CARNOUSTIE *is not
to be persuaded. He hesitates, and finally draws a little away*)

(*With a trace of apology*) I ha'e a slight cold in me heid.
ALBERT (*tactlessly*) You've got cold feet.

EMMA. Instead of talking nonsense, have either of you two got half a crown? (*To Daphne*) That was what you wanted, wasn't it?
DAPHNE. Yes; so silly of me. I *had* to get a taxi from the station and the silly taximan had no change.
ALBERT (*feeling in his pockets*) No, I'm afraid not. Carnoustie . . .?
CARNOUSTIE. Eh?
ALBERT (*crossing below Daphne to* L *of Carnoustie*) Half a croon, quick.
CARNOUSTIE (*faint-heartedly feeling in his pocket*) I don't think I've got it.
ALBERT. Come on!

(CARNOUSTIE *reluctantly produces half a crown and hands it to Albert*)

That's better. There we are. (*He hands the coin to Daphne*)
DAPHNE. Thanks a lot. Remind me to give it you back, won't you?
CARNOUSTIE (*staggered*) Remind you! (*Definitely*) Don't worry, I *wull*.

(DAPHNE *hands the coin to Emma*)

DAPHNE (*with an easy smile*) Do you mind giving that to the man, Aunt Emma?

(EMMA *is about to exit before she recalls herself*)

EMMA. Albert! (*She gives the coin to Albert and nods towards the door* L)
ALBERT. O.K., Ma.

(ALBERT *exits* L)

DAPHNE (*to Carnoustie*) I didn't quite catch your name, I'm afraid.
CARNOUSTIE. Nae one everr does. (*Slowly*) Ma firrst name is Carr-noust-ie.
DAPHNE (*moving down* R) That's a lovely name. (*She puts her handbag, stole and gloves on the chair down* R) But it's a bit of a mouthful, isn't it? (*She looks in the mirror, removes her hat and puts it on the chair*)
CARNOUSTIE. Ma intimate frriends ha'e been known to ca' me "Carrrnie".
DAPHNE (*smiling*) That's much better.
CARNOUSTIE. But I don't approve of it myself.
DAPHNE. Oh. (*To Emma*) Albert's charming, isn't he, Aunt Emma? I'm sure he'll make Shirley very happy.
EMMA (*crossing and standing up* R *of the table* C) Are you? And how's your mother keeping?

(CARNOUSTIE *moves up* LC.
ALBERT *enters* L *and sits on the left arm of the settee*)

DAPHNE. Oh, she's better, much better. But ever so disappointed she couldn't come to the wedding. Aunt Emma . . .?
EMMA. What?
DAPHNE. Would you mind—I'm just dying for a cup of tea. (*She looks in the mirror and pats her hair*)
EMMA. A cup of tea!

(EDIE *enters* R. *She carries a tray of crockery*)

DAPHNE (*turning*) Aunt Edie!
EDIE. Little Daphne! (*She automatically thrusts the tray at Emma*)

(EMMA, *having no option, angrily takes the tray and puts it on the table* C)

(*She moves to Daphne and embraces her*) My—you do look different.
DAPHNE. It's four years since you last saw me, Aunt Edie.
EDIE. And a lovely little girl you were, Daphne lamb.
EMMA (*tersely*) We all change.

(EMMA *exits* R)

EDIE. You've met Albert and Carnegie, haven't you?
DAPHNE. Oh, yes. But where's Shirley and Uncle Henry?
EDIE (*moving above the table*) Shirley'll be back any time now. (*She takes two mats from the tray and lays them on the table*) She's just gone to have her hair done. And your uncle's outside with his ferrets.
DAPHNE (*moving towards the door* R) I'll go and . . . (*She stops*) No, I . . . (*She collects her handbag*) Do you think it'd be all right if I went upstairs for a wash?
EDIE. Yes, of course, love.
DAPHNE. I'm sure I must look awful.
EDIE. You know your way, don't you?
DAPHNE (*crossing towards her case*) Oh—and, Aunt Edie, I've brought you a little present.

(CARNOUSTIE *sits on the settee at the right end*)

(*She picks up the case, puts it on the chair* L *of the table, opens it, takes out a small parcel and gives it to Edie. To Albert*) You're not seeing yours till Shirley gets back.
EDIE (*delighted*) Oh, Daphne, you shouldn't have bothered.
DAPHNE. It's your favourite scent, Auntie. Californian Poppy.
EDIE (*overwhelmed*) Thank you, Daphne. (*She is about to kiss Daphne*)
EMMA (*off; calling*) Edie! You've forgotten the knives and forks.
EDIE (*fluttering*) I'm coming, Emma. (*To Daphne*) I . . . (*She*

puts the parcel in the sideboard drawer) But, perhaps one of the boys would carry your bag up for you?

(EDIE *darts out* R)

DAPHNE (*glancing at the case*) Would one of you . . .? (*She puts her handbag on the table* C)

ALBERT (*rising and crossing to* C) Certainly, it will be a pleasure. (*He picks up the case, the lid falls open and the contents spill on to the floor down* C)

(CARNOUSTIE *rises and moves down* L)

DAPHNE (*moving between Albert and Carnoustie; with a little shriek*) Oh, my things . . .

(ALBERT *and* CARNOUSTIE *gaze at the "things", which are mostly very delightful and intriguing articles of underwear*)

ALBERT. Blimey! Stand back, eager! (*He kneels, picks up the garments and looks at them*)
DAPHNE. Well! Aren't you careless?
ALBERT. I don't know about that. But I'm certainly curious. (*He holds up a transparent nightdress*) You gettin' married, too?
CARNOUSTIE. Albert, I'm shamed.
DAPHNE. There's nothing to be shamed about.

(ALBERT *carefully puts some garments into the case*)

(*She kneels and indignantly hustles other articles into the case. To Carnoustie*) Come on, lend a hand. Come on.

(CARNOUSTIE *bends reluctantly and picks up a brassiere*)

Damn! (*She rises*) I've laddered my nylon. (*She draws her skirt well up above her knee and examines her stocking*)

(*Proximity to Daphne's leg makes* CARNOUSTIE *break* L. *He realizes what the brassiere is and, embarrassed, hides it behind his back*)

Pass me my bag, please, Albert.
ALBERT. Come and sit down—let's have a look. (*He hands Daphne her bag*) Can I help at all?

(DAPHNE *sits* R *of the table* C, *takes her ladder stop from the bag and dabs at her stocking.* ALBERT *sits on the downstage edge of the table* C)

DAPHNE. No, you can't. Just look . . .

(ALBERT *is hopefully about to inspect the damage as the door* L *opens.*

SHIRLEY HORNETT *sails into the room. She is aged about twenty-two and is pretty without Daphne's glamour. She is a pleasant-natured girl, but occasionally one sees "Emma" coming out in her*)

SHIRLEY (*taking in what appears to be the "situation" and not liking it*) Well!

ALBERT ⎫ (*together*)   ⎧Shirl! (*He jumps to his feet*)
DAPHNE ⎭   ⎨Shirley!

(CARNOUSTIE, *still holding the brassiere, merely stands looking at Shirley*)

ALBERT ⎫   ⎧Sweetheart! (*He moves up* C)
DAPHNE ⎬(*together*)   ⎨I can't get up for a minute, darling, I've
       ⎭   ⎩   laddered my nylon.

(SHIRLEY *crosses below Albert and above the table to* R *of Daphne and pecks her right cheek.* ALBERT *moves to* R *of* SHIRLEY *and kisses her, but she soon pushes him away up* RC)

SHIRLEY (*rather hoity-toity*) I'm sorry if I've interrupted something. How are you, Daphne? (*She moves to the chair down* R *and puts her gloves and bag on it*) Having fun, aren't you? (*She sniffs, then turns to look at Carnoustie*)

ALBERT (*moving to* L *of Shirley and putting his arm around her*) Oh, Shirl, it's good to see you again.

SHIRLEY (*releasing herself*) Albert, aren't you going to introduce me? (*She looks towards Carnoustie*)

ALBERT. Of course, Shirley, this is Carnoustie—I've told you about him in my letters. Carnoustie Bligh. (*He moves above Daphne*) Carnoustie—Shirley.

(SHIRLEY *crosses below the table to Carnoustie and holds out her hand*)

SHIRLEY (*rather icily*) How do you do?

CARNOUSTIE (*holding the brassiere in his left hand and shaking hands with the other*) How d'ye do?

SHIRLEY (*after giving him a wan smile*) It's all right, Mr Bligh— (*with a wave of the hand to the brassiere*) you can finish dressing. (*She crosses to the door* R *and calls*) Mum, I'm back.

(CARNOUSTIE, *after Shirley's taunt, glares at the brassiere, almost dancing with rage, flings it into Daphne's case and sits on the settee*)

(*She moves down* R) Well, this *is* a surprise. You weren't supposed to be arriving till half-past six. I was coming down to the station to meet you.

ALBERT (*moving to Shirley and putting an arm around her*) We got an earlier train.

SHIRLEY (*icy towards Albert*) How long have you been here?

ALBERT. About twenty minutes.

SHIRLEY (*with meaning*) Daphne been here all that time, too? How's Auntie Kate, Daphne?

DAPHNE (*still fixing the ladder; with a little bite in her tone*) I got here five minutes ago, and mum's very well, thank you very much.

SHIRLEY (*to Daphne*) If I'd known *you* were here, I'd have got back sooner.

DAPHNE (*dabbing her stocking; half muttering*) I'll bet you would.

(ALBERT *kisses Shirley*)

ALBERT. Shirley, I thought you were never coming.

SHIRLEY (*with a glance at Daphne*) You seem to have been passing the time very pleasantly.

ALBERT. Oh—darling! (*He embraces her*)

SHIRLEY (*releasing herself; petulantly*) Albert! My hair! I've just had it done. (*She turns to the mirror and tidies her hair*) I want it to look *something* like tomorrow.

(DAPHNE *rises, replaces the ladder stopper in her handbag and takes a parcel from her suitcase*)

DAPHNE (*crossing and handing the parcel to Shirley*) From mum and me. With all our love and best wishes for your future happiness together.

SHIRLEY (*after a tiny pause while she struggles with her better nature; smiling*) Thank you, Daphne. (*She gives Daphne a genuine kiss*)

ALBERT (*moving to* L *of Daphne*) Thank you, Daphne.

(ALBERT *is about to kiss her, but the wise* DAPHNE *grabs his hand and shakes it heartily.* SHIRLEY's *eyes are on the parcel she is holding*)

Oh, yes—(*after a quick look towards Shirley; quietly*) I see what you mean.

SHIRLEY. M'mm?

ALBERT. Nothing, darling.

SHIRLEY. Shall we open it now?

(DAPHNE *collects her bag, hat, stole and gloves and crosses to* R *of the sofa*)

DAPHNE (*tactfully*) Wait till I'm out of the room. (*She indicates her case and moves to the door* L. *To Carnoustie*) Do you mind?

CARNOUSTIE (*stupidly*) No' in the least.

DAPHNE. If you would be so good?

(*As* CARNOUSTIE *still looks blank,* ALBERT *gestures to him.* CARNOUSTIE *still looks blank.* ALBERT *gestures again.* CARNOUSTIE *sees the light*)

CARNOUSTIE (*rising and picking up Daphne's case*) Och—I comprrrehend. (*He moves to the door* L) You two want to be left alone, eh?

(DAPHNE *giggles and exits* L.

CARNOUSTIE *follows her off.* SHIRLEY *puts the parcel on the table* C)

ALBERT (*now they are alone*) Darling!
SHIRLEY. Oh, Albert!

(*They go into a big embrace.*
  EDIE *enters* R, *carrying some knives and forks. She sees the embrace and hastily exits*)

ALBERT (*at last*) Happy?
SHIRLEY (*moving below the table* C) I don't know. I was—until I came in just now and saw you—and Daphne—and that—disgusting Scotchman you've brought with you.
ALBERT. Disgusting? Carnoustie? What's there disgusting about him?
SHIRLEY. Standing there, holding Daphne's—er—thingummy-bobs in his hand as bold as brass. (*She works herself up a little*) Yes, and you were as bad, if not worse. Heaven only knows what *you* were up to.
ALBERT (*moving to* R *of Shirley*) Now wait a minute. You don't understand. You see, Daphne's suitcase burst open, and . . .
SHIRLEY. But I blame Daphne as much as either of you. She's clever. She can lead any man astray.
ALBERT. She'll be *damned* clever if she leads Carnoustie.
SHIRLEY (*moving to the settee*) But when I see you carrying on like that, it frightens me. It makes me wonder whether, perhaps, mother isn't right, after all, in what she says.
ALBERT. What does she say?
SHIRLEY. She's always rubbing it in about you being a sailor, and "you know what sailors are—a girl in every port".
ALBERT (*moving to her*) Shirl, you don't believe that about me, do you?
SHIRLEY (*petulantly*) Well, I've tried not to, but when I see you carrying on like that—(*she sits on the settee at the left end*) the day before your wedding, too—well, it just makes me wonder, that's all.
ALBERT. Listen, Shirley. (*He sits* R *of her on the settee*) I give you my word of honour there was nothing wrong. Well, how *could* we, anyway, with your mother and Aunt Edie bobbing in and out all the time?
SHIRLEY (*rising; nattering*) I see! So, if it hadn't been for them bobbing in and out, as you call it, anything might have happened. Is that it?
ALBERT (*rising; patiently*) Listen, darling . . :
SHIRLEY. It's perhaps as well I came in when I did.
ALBERT (*suddenly snapping*) P'raps it *is*. Five more minutes and we might all have been rolling stark naked on the hearth-rug.

(SHIRLEY *dissolves into tears*)

SHIRLEY (*with a slow, rising wail*) Oh, Al-bert!

ALBERT (*penitent immediately*) Sweetheart—I didn't mean . . .
(*He puts his arms around her*)
SHIRLEY (*weeping loudly in his arms*) Oh—Al-bert—lend me
your handkerchief.

(ALBERT *gives* SHIRLEY *his handkerchief and she weeps louder than
ever.*

EMMA *enters* R. *She carries a tray with plates, cruet, etc.*)

EMMA (*as she enters*) Now what . . .? (*She puts the tray on the
table* C *and transfers the contents to the table. With great satisfaction*)
Aaah! This is a *fine* kick-off, isn't it? What have I always said?
And if he has you crying your eyes out on your wedding eve,
what's he going to do when he's been married to you for five
years?

ALBERT (*crossing to* L *of the table; desperately*) You've got it all
wrong, Ma. It was just a little misunderstanding.

EMMA (*gloating*) Little misunderstanding, eh? There'll be lot
more little misunderstandings *very* soon, if I'm any judge. Little
misunderstanding about what, may I ask? (*She puts the empty tray
on the floor* R *of the sideboard*)

SHIRLEY (*calming down a little*) It was nothing, Ma——

ALBERT (*snapping lightly at Emma*) And anyway, it doesn't
concern you.

EMMA (*moving to* R *of the table* C; *snapping at Albert*) Don't you
talk to me like that. (*She sets out the cups and saucers*) Telling me my
own daughter's 'appiness doesn't concern me.

ALBERT. I didn't mean . . .

EMMA. She isn't your wife, yet, remember. (*She moves above the
table and puts the teaspoons in the saucers*)

SHIRLEY. Stop picking on Albert, Mother.

EMMA. That's right. Now you start on me.

ALBERT. Listen, Ma; if you'll just leave us alone for two
minutes . . .

EMMA. You can settle your differences later on if you don't
mind. We've got to get the table laid. Seeing you're all here, we
might as well get tea over and done with. (*She calls*) Edie.

EDIE (*off; calling*) Coming, Emma.

EMMA (*looking around*) Where's Daphne?

SHIRLEY. She's gone upstairs.

EMMA. And where's—Car—(*to Albert*) that friend of yours?

ALBERT. Carnoustie's gone with her.

EMMA. *What!*

ALBERT. I mean, he's taken her bag up for her.

(EDIE *enters* R. *She carries some knives and forks which she sets out
round the table.* EMMA *sets out the paper napkins*)

EMMA (*sharply*) Shirley—(*she points to the door* L) go upstairs—
look after Daphne.

SHIRLEY. But, Mum . . .

EMMA (*quickly*) Shirley 'Ornett!

SHIRLEY (*after a shrug of the shoulders*) O.K. (*She smiles at Albert, collects her handbag and gloves and crosses to the door* L)

ALBERT (*trying to be cheerful*) Shall I be opening the parcel, Shirl? (*He picks up the parcel*)

SHIRLEY (*remembering*) Oh, yes, do.

(SHIRLEY *exits* L)

EMMA (*nattering*) "Shirl"! What's the matter with "Shirley"? (*She moves down* L) It's the name she was given at her baptism. (*With a snort*) "Shirl", indeed!

(ALBERT *looks at Emma for a moment, but decides to say nothing. He tussles with the string of the parcel*)

What's that you've got there?

ALBERT (*down* R) It's a wedding present from Daphne and her mum.

EMMA (*crossing to Albert*) Here, give it to me. I'll undo it for you.

ALBERT (*removing the string*) It's all right, Ma; I've done it.

EMMA (*taking the parcel from him and moving to* R *of the table*) Men never could undo parcels properly. (*With her back to Albert, she removes the wrappings and produces a rose bowl from the box*) H'mm! Oh, Edie, isn't that nice?

(ALBERT *endeavours to see what was in the parcel*)

EDIE (*moving to* L *of Emma*) Oh, it's beautiful! Isn't it, Albert?

ALBERT (*standing on tiptoes for a moment and looking over Emma's shoulder*) Lovely!

EMMA (*putting the bowl on the sideboard*) We'll put it here until Shirley's seen it and then it can go with all the other presents. (*She hands the box, paper and string to Edie*) Here, Edie, take this out into the kitchen and tell Henry to leave those blessed ferrets and come in here.

(EDIE *exits with alacrity* R)

(*She looks at the table*) Now, let me see . . . Oh, yes. Bread and butter.

(EMMA *exits* R. ALBERT *stands looking after her for a moment, then moves slowly to the sideboard, looks at the rose bowl for a moment, picks it up, holds it in both hands and stands quite still, thinking. He then gives a big sigh, replaces the bowl and gazes out of the window.*

CARNOUSTIE *enters* L *and wanders to* L *of Albert. He does not look very happy*)

CARNOUSTIE. Hi!

(ALBERT *pats Carnoustie on the shoulder and smiles a little wanly at him*)

ALBERT. How are you, son?

(CARNOUSTIE *tries to smile.*
HENRY *enters* R)

HENRY (*cheerfully*) Hullo, there. (*He moves to the fireplace*)
ALBERT (*equally cheerfully*) 'Lo, Pop.
HENRY (*picking up his slippers from the hearth and sitting in the armchair; a little apprehensively*) Everything all right? (*He removes his boots and dons his slippers*)
ALBERT (*crossing to the fireplace*) Fine, thanks, Pop, fine.
HENRY. That's right. (*To Carnoustie*) Tea'll be in in a minute. (*To Albert*) Gettin' nervous, Albert?

(CARNOUSTIE *moves to the settee and sits*)

ALBERT. Nervous?
HENRY. 'Bout tomorrow.
ALBERT. I . . . (*He abruptly changes the subject and turns away down* R) How are your ferrets keeping, Pop?
HENRY (*blinking*) Eh? (*The sudden change of subject bewilders him for a moment*) Ferrets? Oh, they're fine, Albert. You must come and have a look at 'em after tea. I've just been cleaning 'em out.
ALBERT. Thanks, Pop, I'd like to.
HENRY (*rising and crossing to the door* L; *with a side-glance at Albert*) Good! Well, I'll just pop upstairs and have a wash.

(EMMA *enters* R. *She carries a plate of bread and butter which she puts on the table* C)

EMMA (*as she enters*) Henry, I thought I told you to go up and wash.
HENRY (*opening the door* L; *with a touch of irritation*) I'm just going.
EMMA. I don't know what you want to go messin' about with them smelly things for, just before tea-time. (*She points to Henry's boots*) And them boots don't belong there.
HENRY (*crossing to the fireplace; to Albert*) Wait till you've a woman chasin' you around—(*he picks up his boots*) then you'll know you're born.

(HENRY *exits* R. EMMA *puts milk into the cups*)

EMMA. I only hope Shirley puts her foot down right from the start. You'll take a bit of keeping in order if all I hear about sailors is true.

(HENRY *enters* R *and crosses towards the door* L)

HENRY. I'm just going to have my wash.

EMMA (*pointing to the armchair*) You'll put that jacket where it belongs, first.

HENRY (*crossing to the armchair; impatiently*) Well, for the Lord's sake . . .

(HENRY *breaks off, remembering the presence of the boys. He picks up his jacket, tie and collar, crosses and exits* L. ALBERT *has not been unaware of all the foregoing. When Henry has gone, he produces a packet of cigarettes, slowly extracts one and puts it in his mouth*)

EMMA. You don't have to go lighting cigarettes. Tea'll be in in a minute.

(EMMA *exits* R. ALBERT, *with no sign of irritation, replaces the cigarette and puts the packet in his pocket. Almost unconsciously he whistles the first four lines of "A Life on the Ocean Wave". Then he turns his head and looks at* CARNOUSTIE, *who turns and looks at Albert.* ALBERT *crosses and sits on the settee,* R *of Carnoustie*)

ALBERT (*patting Carnoustie's knee; automatically*) How are you, son?

(SHIRLEY *enters* L, *moves behind the settee, affectionately ruffles Albert's hair and kisses the top of his head*)

SHIRLEY (*her ill-humour gone*) Hello, darling.

(ALBERT *is, at once, all smiles again.* CARNOUSTIE *rises from the settee to make room for Shirley*)

CARNOUSTIE. Och, I'm sorry . . .

SHIRLEY (*moving below the settee*) No, don't move. (*She smiles and sits on Albert's knee*) Car-nous-tie. That's right, isn't it?

CARNOUSTIE (*resuming his seat*) Aye, that's right.

SHIRLEY. I like it. But it takes a bit of remembering. (*To Carnoustie*) I—I'm sorry if I was a bit snappy when I came in just now . . .

CARNOUSTIE (*blushing with embarrassment*) Och! No, no, you werena' . . .

SHIRLEY. Oh, Albert, I wish you had a lovely Scotch accent like that.

CARNOUSTIE (*more embarrassed*) Och—you're only saying that —because it's true.

SHIRLEY (*to Carnoustie*) I don't wonder Daphne's fallen for you in such a big way.

CARNOUSTIE (*realizing what Shirley has said*) What!

SHIRLEY. But I warned her.

CARNOUSTIE. Warrrned her about wha'?

SHIRLEY. You. It's the quiet ones like your sort that do the damage.

CARNOUSTIE. I've never done anyone damage in ma life.

ALBERT. Then it's high time you began.

(EMMA *enters* R. *She carries a pot of tea which she puts on the table.*

  EDIE *enters* R. *She carries a bowl of salad and a plate of sliced meat which she puts on the table*)

EMMA (*as she enters; almost affably*) Now come on, everyone. Get your teas.

(SHIRLEY, ALBERT *and* CARNOUSTIE *rise.*
  EDIE *exits* R)

Bring your chairs up. (*She goes to the door* L *and calls*) Daphne. Henry. Tea's in.

(DAPHNE *and* HENRY, *linked arm in arm, enter* L. HENRY *stands by the shelves up* L *and fiddles with the gong.* EMMA, ALBERT, CARNOUSTIE *and* DAPHNE *bring chairs to the table. There are two chairs above the table, two chairs* L *of it and two chairs* R *of it*)

Now, let's see. (*She indicates the chair above the right end of the table*) Albert, you sit there—(*she looks at Carnoustie*) and—(*she cannot get the name*) you sit next to him.

(ALBERT *sits above the right end of the table.* CARNOUSTIE *sits* R *of the table on the upstage chair*)

Shirley, there in your usual place. (*She indicates the downstage chair* L *of the table, a long way from Albert*)
SHIRLEY (*protesting*) Oh, but, Mother, can't I sit next to Albert?
EMMA. You'll have plenty of time for holding hands after tomorrow. (*She indicates the downstage chair* R *of the table, next to Carnoustie*) Sit you down, Daphne, over there.

(SHIRLEY *sits* L *of the table on the downstage chair.* DAPHNE *sits* R *of the table on the downstage chair.* CARNOUSTIE *edges his chair close to Albert, bending away from Daphne as if he feared she was going to attack him.* DAPHNE *edges her chair close to Carnoustie*)

DAPHNE (*to Carnoustie*) It's all right. I've got a slight cold in the head, myself.

(EDIE *enters* R. *She carries a stool which she places below the table*)

EMMA. Henry, what are you dithering about at? Come and sit down, do. And you, too, Edie. Come on.

(HENRY *sits on the upstage chair* L *of the table*)

EDIE (*fluttering*) I was just wondering if there was anything else wanted from the kitchen. (*She sits on the stool*)
SHIRLEY. Help yourself, won't you, Carnoustie? And you, Albert.

(EDIE *serves the meat.* EMMA, *standing, pours six cups of tea.*

(HENRY *and* ALBERT *pass the cups.* ALBERT *passes a cup to Daphne, takes one for himself and passes an empty cup to Carnoustie.* HENRY *passes a cup to Edie, a cup to Shirley, and takes one for himself.* ALBERT *helps himself to salad.* HENRY *tucks his paper napkin into his collar*)

EMMA. You'll all have to help yourselves. We don't stand on ceremony here—(*in the same breath*) Henry, you don't need that thing stuck down your throat. (*She snatches Henry's napkin and puts it in his lap*) How many times do I have to tell you about that trick? (*She sits* L *of Albert above the table*) Don't let me catch you doing it at the reception tomorrow, either—(*in the same breath*) everybody 'appy?

(*The meal proceeds.* CARNOUSTIE *places the salad bowl between himself and Daphne*)

DAPHNE. Shirley tells me you're not having the reception here, Aunt Emma? (*She helps herself to salad*)

EMMA. No, we're not. We haven't the room for one thing. Much better having it at *Banfields Tea Rooms*. They've got a nice big place for functions.

DAPHNE. How many *are* coming, Shirley?

EMMA. About thirty, as far as we know. But there's bound to be some unexpecteds. There usually is.

DAPHNE. Many on your side, Albert?

ALBERT. No—I—I haven't anybody to come. Not a soul.

(CARNOUSTIE *coughs*)

Except Carnoustie, of course.

(CARNOUSTIE *looks embarrassed.* EDIE *serves Emma with meat.* CARNOUSTIE *helps himself to salad.* EMMA *offers the sugar basin around*)

DAPHNE (*gazing at Carnoustie*) Oh.

(HENRY *holds the salad bowl while* EMMA *helps herself to salad*)

SHIRLEY. Albert's an orphan, Daphne. Aren't you, Albert?

ALBERT. That's right. An orphan of the storm.

(EDIE *suddenly gives a little sniff, and quickly dabs her eyes with her handkerchief.* SHIRLEY *holds the bowl while* HENRY *helps himself to salad*)

EMMA (*to Edie*) Now then, Edie, don't you start.

EDIE. I'm sorry, Emma. It was just thinking of poor Albert being an orphan of the storm and having nobody at the wedding.

(SHIRLEY *helps herself to salad*)

ALBERT (*cheerfully*) Don't you worry about me, Aunt Edie. I'll be all right. Besides, you'll be there to back me up, won't you?

EDIE. I—I . . . (*She jumps up quickly and dabs her eyes*) 'Scuse me.

(EDIE *exits hurriedly* R)

EMMA (*almost snapping at Albert*) Now what did you have to go and say that for?
ALBERT (*mystified*) Say what?
EMMA. About her going to the wedding.
ALBERT. Well, what . . .?
SHIRLEY. Aunt Edie isn't going, Albert. (*She passes the salad to Daphne*)

(DAPHNE *puts the salad bowl in front of Edie's place*)

ALBERT. Not going?
SHIRLEY. No, you see she—she doesn't want to. You see . . .
EMMA (*sharply*) All right—all right. We won't go over all that if you don't mind. Henry, pass—that lad—some bread.

(HENRY *passes the bread and butter to Carnoustie*)

ALBERT. But why doesn't she want . . .?
EMMA (*firmly*) I said we wouldn't talk about that now, if you don't mind. Now do get on with your teas, everybody. There's a lot to be done tonight, yet.

(*The door* R *opens*)

(*Loudly*) Ssssh!

(EDIE *enters* R. *She has regained control and carries a jug of hot water which she puts on the table*)

EDIE (*with just a little sniff; awkwardly*) I've brought you some hot water, Emma. (*She resumes her seat*)
EMMA. Thank you, we could do with it.

(ALBERT *lifts the lid of the teapot while* EMMA *puts water in it. The meal proceeds in a rather obvious silence, which everyone would like to break, but no one does.* EDIE *sips her tea. Everyone is tucking in, except* CARNOUSTIE *who fidgets with his empty cup*)

CARNOUSTIE (*presently and practically*) Could I have a cup of tea with my tea? (*He rises*)

(*The sound of Carnoustie's voice makes everyone jump*)

EMMA (*recovering*) Eh?
CARNOUSTIE (*remembering his manners*) Please. (*He resumes his seat*)
EMMA. Pass your cup.

(CARNOUSTIE *passes his cup. The tension is now broken*)

(*She pours tea for Carnoustie*) And when you've had your tea, Henry, you'd better go upstairs and have your bath; then the water will get nice and hot for me to have one before I go to bed. (*She passes the cup of tea to Carnoustie*)

HENRY. But I . . .

(EDIE *helps herself to salad*)

EMMA (*sweeping on*) We can't all have baths in the morning so you and me'll have ours tonight and Albert and—(*she has a shot at it*) Carminskie here—can have one next door, I expect.

HENRY. Yes, but what I thought . . .

EMMA. Now don't start making trouble. I've got quite enough on my mind. Shirley, there's a lot to be done tonight for you and me and Edie.

DAPHNE. Can I help, Aunt Emma?

EMMA. Yes, Daphne, you can. (*To Albert*) And you boys'll just have to sit back and keep out of the way.

ALBERT. Well, as a matter of fact, we've arranged to go out, Ma.

EMMA (*immediately disapproving*) What?

ALBERT. Yes. And we're going to ask Pop to come with us, too.

EMMA. Going out—where?

ALBERT. Couple of lads from our ship live here—as a matter of fact they travelled up on the same train as us—and we arranged to meet 'em at the *White Hart* at eight o'clock.

SHIRLEY (*petulantly*) Oh, Albert!

ALBERT (*pleasantly*) Well, what's wrong, Shirl? You've got a lot to do, and Ma's just said we'd have to keep out of the way.

SHIRLEY. Yes, but . . .

EMMA. Well, of course, you'll suit yourselves, but it seems a pity to me if all you can think about the night before your wedding is drinking.

ALBERT (*still pleasantly*) It isn't the drink so much, Ma; but it'll be nice to see the lads.

EMMA. See the . . .! Good Lord, you haven't left them an hour since.

ALBERT. I know that, but—we won't be long. We'll be back by nine or half past.

HENRY. Yes. And after all, Emma, it is his last night of freedom.

ALBERT (*startled by the remark*) Eh?

HENRY. Oh, I know you've got your three months more service to do, but after that . . .

EMMA. After that—what?

HENRY (*uncomfortably*) Well . . .

EMMA. Anyone would think he was going to prison, to hear you talk.

HENRY (*uncomfortably*) Well . . .

DAPHNE. Can I have a piece of bread and butter, Aunt Emma, please?

EMMA (*her mind still on Henry*) Help yourself.

(DAPHNE *tries to reach the bread and butter, but cannot.* ALBERT *takes bread and butter*)

(*To Henry*) I only hope Albert here has half such a cosy time in his married life as *you've* had in yours, and I hope he'll show poor Shirley a bit more appreciation than you've ever shown me.

HENRY (*wearily*) Now don't start bringing that up again. You've been telling me how lucky I've been practically since the day we were married. All right, if it pleases you, I'll take your word for it. Pass the mustard.

EMMA. That's quite enough out of you. (*To Albert*) So that's settled, then, you're stopping in.

SHIRLEY. Yes, of course they are, Mum. Now let's stop this bickering, for goodness' sake.

ALBERT. But, Shirl . . .

SHIRLEY. Now what?

ALBERT. Listen, what's the point of our staying in? *You* won't have time to be bothered with us—none of you.

SHIRLEY (*plaintively*) Well, that isn't my fault, is it?

ALBERT. I know that—I'm not grumbling. I realize how . . .

SHIRLEY. If you knew how much there is to be done before tomorrow morning . . .

ALBERT. Well, all right, look, can *I* do anything if I *do* stay?

SHIRLEY. No, Albert, they're not the kind of things you *could* do.

ALBERT (*with the slightest touch of annoyance*) Then, why not let Pop, Carnoustie and me get out of the way while you do them?

EMMA (*really snapping now*) I should have thought that if Shirley says she wants you here, that would have been enough.

ALBERT. But, Ma . . .

EMMA. Isn't it natural she should want you here?

ALBERT. No, not if we're going to be in the way, it's not.

EDIE. Emma—I don't want to interfere . . .

EMMA. Then don't! (*To Albert*) Shirley doesn't want you going out getting drunk the minute you get here.

CARNOUSTIE (*rising*) Mrs Hornett, I've never been drunk in ma life.

EMMA. I'm talking to Albert, Carnaskie.

(CARNOUSTIE *resumes his seat*)

SHIRLEY. I never said anything about them getting drunk, Mum. It's just that . . .

ALBERT. That what?

SHIRLEY (*snapping*) Well, I think you ought to stay in, that's all. If Carnoustie wants to go . . .

CARNOUSTIE. I must. I promised the lads I'd go.

SHIRLEY (*rising and crossing quickly to the fireplace; near to tears*) Well, Albert, I suppose you'll do what you think best, but . . .

HENRY (*helping himself to bread and butter*) If he has any sense he will.

EMMA. You keep quiet. You've said quite enough. But I'll tell you one thing—whether Albert goes or not, *you're* not going.

DAPHNE (*holding out her cup*) Can I have another cup of tea, please, Aunt Emma?

(EMMA *ignores* DAPHNE, *who puts down her cup*)

EMMA (*to Henry*) I can find you plenty to do here without your going down to the pub, drinking. Heaven knows it's little enough interest you've taken in your daughter's wedding, so far. Shirley, come and sit down and finish your tea.

SHIRLEY. I don't want any more. I'm too upset.

ALBERT (*rising and moving to Shirley*) Now listen, Shirl . . .

SHIRLEY. I don't want to listen, Albert. I know how I feel about it, and that's that. If you want to go, go.

EMMA (*rising*) That's no way to talk. It's just giving in to him.

HENRY (*half rising; to Emma*) Now can't you keep your mouth shut.

EMMA. 'Enry 'Ornett!

(HENRY *resumes his seat*)

ALBERT. Go and sit down, Shirl; there's a good girl.

SHIRLEY. But, Albert . . .

ALBERT (*firmly*) Go and sit down.

(SHIRLEY, *after a sniff, resumes her seat at the table*)

DAPHNE (*holding out her cup*) Can I have another cup of tea, please, Aunt Emma?

EMMA (*picking up the teapot; to Albert*) Well, have you made up your mind what you're going to do?

ALBERT. Yes.

EMMA. What?

ALBERT (*moving to the table*) Finish my tea. (*He resumes his seat*)

(EMMA *sits and pours tea for Daphne.* HENRY *rises and moves up* R)

HENRY (*to Albert; firmly*) Yes, and if you have any sense, lad, you'll do what you want to do. Don't make the mistake I did, or you won't be able to call your soul your own.

EMMA (*rising furiously, teapot in hand*) 'Enry 'Ornett!

HENRY (*moving to the door* R) I'm going out to my ferrets.

(HENRY *exits* R, *slamming the door behind him.* EMMA *puts the teapot on the sideboard, goes to the door* R *and opens it*)

EMMA (*calling*) 'Enry 'Ornett! You'll come back here this minute, or I'll come and . . .

B

Edie (*with a scream*) Emma! The teapot. (*She rises*)

Emma (*spinning round*) What!

Edie (*rushing to the sideboard*) The sideboard . . .

Emma (*almost overlapping*) Oh, my . . .

Emma *reaches the sideboard at the same time as* Edie *and grabs the teapot as—*

the Curtain *falls*

ACT II

SCENE 1

SCENE—*The same. Nine-thirty the same evening.*

When the CURTAIN *rises, the window curtains are closed and the light is on.* EMMA, EDIE, SHIRLEY *and* DAPHNE *are hovering around a large tea-chest down* L, *into which they are placing the last of the wedding presents.*

EMMA. Here, wait a minute—there's one more—though what it's supposed to be beats me. You'd better ask Florrie Lack, she gave it to you. (*She wraps the ornament in newspaper and places it in the tea-chest*) Now take that outside and when you're there you might as well make us all a nice cup of tea.

(DAPHNE *and* EDIE *pick up the tea-chest and cross to the door* R. SHIRLEY *sits on the chair down* R)

DAPHNE (*to Edie*) And when we've had our tea I'm going to get you to read my cup.
EDIE. Oh, but . . .
DAPHNE. Now, you know how good you are at it.
EDIE. Yes, but . . . Well, you'll have to ask your Aunt Emma.

(DAPHNE *and* EDIE *exit with the tea-chest* R)

EMMA. Now, Shirley 'Ornett, you can just stop pulling a long face. (*She crosses to the armchair*)
SHIRLEY. Oh, Mother, don't start on me again, please. I can't stand any more of it.
EMMA. That's no way to talk, my girl. "Can't stand any more of it", eh? Then, all I can say is, Lord help you; because as far as I can see your troubles haven't really started yet. (*She sits in the armchair*)
SHIRLEY (*looking at the clock*) If only Albert would come back.
EMMA. You should never have let him go. You should have put your foot down. I *told* you, didn't I?
SHIRLEY (*weeping*) I did put it down; but he went just the same.
EMMA. Well, you'll have to learn to put it down harder. You can't reason with men. You've just got to *train* 'em. That's what I've had to do with your father, and look at the result. He may answer back a bit now and again, same as he did tonight at tea; but he comes to heel all right. He's as happy as a lark fiddling with his ferrets, instead of wasting his money in public houses.
SHIRLEY. I wish you liked Albert a bit more, Mum.

35

EMMA. And *I* wish I knew more about him. No parents, no relations—dragged up in an Orphanage; *and* a sailor into the bargain. What can he know about "home life"?

SHIRLEY. But there's nothing he wants more than to settle down.

EMMA. Well—so long as he *does* settle; but—you know what sailors are. And he hasn't done much settling down tonight, has he? Isn't in the house five minutes before he's off down to the pub drinking. (*She looks at the clock*) Yes, and look at the time. I told Florrie Lack those two would be round at her place at ten o'clock, and not a minute later. And it's well past half-past nine, already.

SHIRLEY. And Albert said he'd be back by nine o'clock. I've got to have a talk with him before he goes to Mrs Lack's. I mustn't see him in the morning, before the wedding, must I?

EMMA. That you mustn't. (*She rises*) Well, I suppose I'd better send your father round to the *White Hart* to fetch him back. Nice start off, isn't it? (*She moves to the door* R *and opens it*)

SHIRLEY. Mum . . .

EMMA (*stopping and turning*) Yes?

SHIRLEY. I—(*she rises*) I haven't said anything to Albert, yet, about—Number Twenty-four.

EMMA (*moving to* L *of the armchair*) Well, why not?

SHIRLEY. Well, after tea, he was talking about us going over to Badcaster when we came back from our honeymoon—and having a look round for a little house, or a flat.

EMMA (*moving down* RC) You should have told him then.

SHIRLEY. I was a bit frightened to.

EMMA. Frightened! There's nothing to be frightened about. Good Lord!

SHIRLEY (*with a step towards Emma*) It's just that—perhaps I ought to have waited till he'd got here, and talked it over with him.

(DAPHNE *and* EDIE *enter* R. DAPHNE *carries a tray with tea things for four which she puts on the table* C. EDIE *carries a pot of tea*)

DAPHNE (*moving to* L *of the table*) Here we are. Shall I pour out, Aunt Emma?

(EDIE *stands by the sideboard*)

MRS LACK (*off* R; *calling*) Are you there, Emma?

EMMA (*sitting* R *of the table*) Now, what . . .?

EDIE. It's only Mrs Lack, Emma.

(MRS LACK *enters* R)

MRS LACK (*crossing below Emma and standing above the table*) That's right, Edie. It's only me.

(SHIRLEY *moves and sits on the settee*)

(*Almost cheerfully*) And I've got bad news. Can I sit down? (*She sits above the table*) We're in a nice mess, now.

EMMA. Why, what's the matter?

MRS LACK. Our Rita.

(EDIE *moves to* L *of Mrs Lack and places the teapot on a mat on the table*)

(*With a show of surprise*) Oh, were you just going to have a cuppa?

EMMA (*shortly*) Fetch another cup and saucer, Edie.

(EDIE *exits* R)

MRS LACK. Oh, don't bother, Emma. Well, thank you very much.

EMMA. What about Rita?

(DAPHNE *pours two cups of tea*)

MRS LACK. Measles!

EMMA. What!

MRS LACK. Measles. She's got 'em.

EMMA. Well, of all the thoughtless, stupid . . . Oh, no!

SHIRLEY. That means she can't be a bridesmaid?

(DAPHNE *passes cups of tea to Emma and Shirley*)

MRS LACK. 'Fraid so, love. You remember, Emma, I told you she stayed away from school this afternoon with a headache? Well, about half an hour ago I heard her calling for me. I went up to her—my God—you should have seen her. 'Orrid, she looked; proper 'orrid. I went across to Nurse Smith, and she just took one look at her and "Measles", she said. Just like that. I *said* to her, "Nurse, it can't be——

(EDIE *enters* R *and moves to* R *of Mrs Lack. She carries a cup and saucer*)

—Rita's got to be a bridesmaid, tomorrow."

EDIE. And a *lovely* bridesmaid she'll be, won't she, Shirley?

MRS LACK. I said to her, "Nurse, can't you do nothing?" And she said, "Not for measles, I can't, Mrs Lack."

(DAPHNE *pours two cups of tea*)

EDIE (*squeaking*) Measles! Rita hasn't got the . . .

EMMA (*snapping*) Edie—you be quiet.

MRS LACK. "Only time will cure them," she said. "Time, warmth and opening medicine. Get the doctor in the morning." So there we are.

(DAPHNE *passes a cup of tea to Mrs Lack*)

Thank you, love. Oh—er—excuse me—(*she indicates that she has not "met" Daphne*) I was so full of my bad news I didn't realize . . .

EMMA (*shortly*) This is Daphne, my sister's girl.

MRS LACK. Oh. You were going to be the *other* bridesmaid with Rita. You'll have to manage on your own, now, won't you? (*She helps herself to sugar*)

DAPHNE. I'll manage. (*She sits* L *of the table* C)

SHIRLEY. Oh, dear! What will it look like—only one bridesmaid.

MRS LACK. And Rita would have looked such a picture. She looked lovely in her dress. 'Course, she wouldn't, all covered with spots, would she?

(EDIE *moves to* L *of Mrs Lack and pours a cup of tea for herself*)

(*After a brief pause*) Then, of course, there's the boys.

EMMA. What boys?

MRS LACK. Why, the bridegroom and his best man.

EMMA. Well, what about them?

MRS LACK. I won't be able to put them up for the night, now.

EMMA (*sharply*) What! Why not? There's no danger of them catching measles.

MRS LACK. No, but you see there's Evadne. (*To Daphne*) That's Rita's sister—she's only five, bless her. (*To Emma*) Well, she always sleeps with Rita; but of course, now I'll have to put her on her own. That means she'll have to go into my spare room, and that's the room I was going to let the lads have.

EMMA. Well, this is a nice how-do-you-do, I must say. *Now* what are we going to do?

MRS LACK. I'm sorry, Emma; but you see how it is, don't you?

EMMA (*shortly*) Yes. I *see*!

MRS LACK. They'll have to go round to the *Rose and Crown* after all. And they'll have to pay there. Twelve and six a night without breakfast, I believe it is. 'Course, I wasn't going to charge 'em quite as much as that.

EMMA. You . . .! Here, give me another cup of tea, Edie, for the Lord's sake.

(EDIE *takes Emma's cup, refills it and returns it to her*)

SHIRLEY. Everything seems to be going wrong, somehow.

MRS LACK. May as well go wrong before as well as after, eh, Emma? Gets you used to it, so to speak. Er . . .

EMMA. I suppose *you* won't be able to go to the wedding, either.

MRS LACK (*horrified at the suggestion*) What! *Me* not there? I'll be there all right. I was going to ask Edie, as she isn't going to the wedding, if she'd mind giving a look in at Rita now and again.

EDIE. Oooh, but I'm going to the *reception*, Mrs Lack. It's just the service I couldn't face. Seein' Shirley standing at the altar, and remembering . . .

MRS LACK (*rather shortly*) Oh, yes. Your "Great Sorrow". We *all* know, don't we, Emma?

EMMA. Edie, if everyone's finished their tea, get the cups and saucers washed up out of the way.

EDIE. Yes, Emma. (*She stacks her own, Emma's and Mrs Lack's cups on the tray*)

EMMA (*rising; to Mrs Lack*) And don't think I'm pushing you off, but—we've a lot to do yet. Thanks for bringing the bad news.

MRS LACK (*rising*) I hope you get the lads fixed up at the *Rose and Crown*. (*Happily*) Though I doubt if you will.

SHIRLEY (*rising; cup in hand*) Shall I slip down there now, Mum?

EMMA. You can stay where you are. I haven't said nothing about any *Rose and Crown*.

(DAPHNE *hands her cup to* EDIE *who gazes into it*)

SHIRLEY. But . . .

(EDIE *suddenly lets out a wail of anguish*)

EDIE (*gazing horrified into the cup*) Ooooooh!

(*They all turn to Edie.* SHIRLEY *puts her cup on the table*)

EMMA		What the . . .?
DAPHNE		Aunt Edie, what's the matter? (*She rises*)
	(*together*)	
MRS LACK		Oh, my!
SHIRLEY		Auntie . . .? (*She moves to* L *of Edie*)

EMMA. Making us all jump out of our skins. What's the matter with you?

EDIE (*pointing to the inside of the cup*) Look!

(*With enquiring "noises", the others crowd around Edie*)

Can you see it?

DAPHNE. What? You mean the tea-leaves?

EMMA (*moving to* L *of the armchair*) Tea-leaves! Is that all?

EDIE. I can see it as plain as daylight. Can't you see it, Mrs Lack? Look—there. (*She points to the inside of the cup. Dramatically*) A bleeding, broken heart!

(SHIRLEY *moves to the window*)

MRS LACK (*stepping back; with a gasp of horror*) Lord save us!

EDIE. I wonder whose it is?

MRS LACK. Let's hope it's yours, Edie.

EDIE (*looking into the cup*) No. It doesn't look like mine.

EMMA (*scornfully*) If it's anybody's, it's mine. My heart broke years ago; but I should have thought it had bled all it was going to by now. (*To Edie*) And now, if you've quite finished cheering us all up, perhaps you'll take those cups and saucers out of here and get 'em washed.

(EDIE, *still shaken by her discovery, stacks the remainder of the cups on the tray, picks it up and exits* R)

You and your . . .

MRS LACK. I wonder if it *was* mine. Well, I'd better be going.

EMMA. Yes, I think you had. If your bleeding heart's going to break, I should let it do it in the comfort of your own home. (*She moves to the fireplace*)

MRS LACK (*moving to the door* R) Well, I'll say, good night, all.

SHIRLEY (*moving up* C) Oh, Mrs Lack—thank you for the wedding present. It—it was just what we wanted.

MRS LACK (*somewhat surprised*) Was it? (*She turns to go. Puzzled*) Good Lord!

(MRS LACK *exits* R)

SHIRLEY (*moving up* R *of the table*) Shall I just slip down to the *Rose and Crown* and see if they have a room?

EMMA. No, you won't. They can sleep here.

SHIRLEY. But, Mum . . .

EMMA. *You* can do with all the spare twelve-and-sixpences that Albert Tufnell has got. There's no need for him to go throwing them away at la-di-da hotels.

SHIRLEY. But where are you going to put them?

EMMA (*pointing to the settee*) On this thing.

DAPHNE (*muttering*) Oh, my . . .! You mean, one at each end?

EMMA. No, I don't. (*She crosses to* L *of the settee*) Here, Shirley, give me a hand. That horrible child would get measles. I never could stand her.

(SHIRLEY *goes to* R *of the settee and helps* EMMA *to open it out as a Put-U-Up*)

DAPHNE. Oh, it's one of those things.

EMMA (*to Shirley*) Yes, it is, and if those two don't like it—they can go and sleep with your father's ferrets, for all I care. *Now,* I suppose, we've got to start finding blankets. A nice time of night to start *that.*

SHIRLEY. I'll help you, Mum.

EMMA. Yes, I should think you will. (*She picks up the two settee cushions*) The sooner you find out what it's like to be slaving your inside out while your husband's drinking himself stupid at the pub, the better. Come on.

(EMMA *exits* L)

DAPHNE. Shall I come, too?

SHIRLEY (*with a nice smile and a wink to Daphne*) No, don't bother. And don't take too much notice of mother. Her bark's worse than her bite.

(SHIRLEY *exits* L)

DAPHNE (*to herself*) But there's such a lot of it. (*She moves to the bed and lies full length on it, thinking. Then she starts to whistle or sing "The Wedding March"*)

(ALBERT *and* CARNOUSTIE *are heard off* L, *singing "Auld Lang Syne"*)

Gosh! (*She rises, moves quickly to the door* L *and peeps off*) Oh, my! (*She closes the door*) Here! Let me get out of this.

(DAPHNE *crosses and exits quickly* R.
ALBERT *peers cautiously round the door* L, *then comes into the room and beckons off. He is without his cap.*
CARNOUSTIE, *with equal caution, enters* L. *He wears his cap*)

ALBERT (*with his finger to his lips*) Sssssh! (*He tiptoes up* C)
CARNOUSTIE (*with his finger to his lips*) Ssssh! (*He closes the door and tiptoes to* L *of Albert*)

(ALBERT *tiptoes up* RC. CARNOUSTIE *moves* C.
HENRY *enters* L. *He is wearing Albert's sailor cap, and is sufficiently drunk to be in a "Don't-care-a-damn" mood*)

HENRY (*singing as he enters*) "And here's a hand—(*he moves between Carnoustie and Albert*) ma trusty friend . . ." (*He raises his right hand*)

(ALBERT *drags Henry's hand down.* HENRY *raises his left hand.* CARNOUSTIE *drags Henry's hand down*)

ALBERT. Ssssh! Pop! Quiet!
HENRY (*grabbing Carnoustie's hand, clinging to him and singing*) "And gie's a hand o' thine."
CARNOUSTIE (*nervously*) Mr Hornett, ye didna ought to . . .
HENRY (*singing him down*) "We'll tak' a cup and drink it up . . ." (*He stops as he realizes the boys are trying to quieten him*) Wassa matter?
CARNOUSTIE (*warningly*) Mrs Hornett!
HENRY (*blinking at him*) Mrs 'Ornett! Pah! (*He pushes the boys aside, goes to the door* L, *flings both arms out with a dramatic gesture and bawls at the very top of his voice*) "For the sake of Auld Lang Syne."

(ALBERT *and* CARNOUSTIE *rush at Henry, each take an arm and drag him from the doorway*)

ALBERT. Pop!
HENRY (*freeing himself; with a big gesture*) Pooh! (*He stands perfectly still for a moment, then, for no reason at all, he shouts*) God save Ould Ireland! (*Immediately, and with amazing agility, he begins*

dancing a hornpipe round the room. What the dance lacks in perfection of execution, it makes up in speed. He simply tears around the room to his own vocal accompaniment)

ALBERT. Cor-blimey! That's done it. (*He runs after Henry, trying to catch him*) Pop!

(EDIE *enters* R)

EDIE (*her eyes popping*) Henry!

(DAPHNE *darts on* R, *grabs* EDIE *by the hand and literally yanks her off* R *again. As he is dancing around,* HENRY *occasionally stretches out a hand and flicks an ornament off the mantelpiece or the sideboard, and immediately returns to the appropriate gestures required for the hornpipe. He flicks an ornament from the downstage end of the mantelpiece but* ALBERT *catches it.* HENRY *flicks an ornament from the upstage end of the mantelpiece; it falls to the floor and breaks. He picks up two ornaments from the sideboard and throws them.* ALBERT *catches one and falls into the armchair;* CARNOUSTIE *catches the other.* ALBERT, *in despair, gives up the chase.* HENRY *flicks an ornament to the floor and it breaks.* ALBERT *shudders, rises, crosses to Carnoustie and almost weeps on his shoulder.* HENRY, *with the hand-over-hand movement, hornpipes backwards towards the door* L.

EMMA *enters* L. *She carries two sheets, a blanket and an eiderdown.* SHIRLEY *is behind Emma. She carries two pillows.* HENRY, *lost in the dance, remains in front of Emma, dancing.* EMMA'S *mouth opens, closes, opens, closes, then when she speaks, the roar of the Bull of Bashan is as the tinkling of fairy bells compared with Emma's voice)*

EMMA. *Henry!*

(HENRY *turns and salutes Emma*)

HENRY. Split your mainbrace! (*He means, of course, "Splice the mainbrace". He recommences the hornpipe, moving down* L, *then down* C)

(EMMA, *her eyes blazing with rage, hurls the bedclothes on to the bed, moves to Henry, grabs him by the lapels, brings him to a standstill, snatches the hat from his head, and flings it away*)

EMMA. You—drunken—sot! (*She gives Henry a vicious shove*)

(HENRY *collapses on to the bed*)

ALBERT (*horrified*) Ma!
CARNOUSTIE (*horrified*) Mrs Hornett!
SHIRLEY. Oh-h!

(SHIRLEY *turns and runs out* L, *taking the pillows with her. There is a pause.* EMMA *turns and faces Albert*)

EMMA (*pointing to Henry*) You did this, didn't you?
ALBERT. I . . . (*He shrugs helplessly and moves below the armchair*)
EMMA. He would never have dared do it off his own bat. You

planned it with him. (*She looks at Henry*) Pretending he was out with his ferrets, when all the time he was . . .

CARNOUSTIE (*firmly*) Here—here—here—here—Albert didna say a worrd to yourr husband aboot comin' doon to the *White Hart*. Ye ha'e ma worrd for that.

EMMA (*menacingly*) So it was you, was it? (*She moves up L of the table* C)

(CARNOUSTIE, *in alarm, moves up* R)

And what gives *you* the right, do you think, to set my husband up in defiance of me? Deliberately persuading him to sneak away behind my back and . . .

CARNOUSTIE. Oh, hey here—Mrs Hornett. I think you're making the mistake of underrating your husband's intelligence.

EMMA. And what do you mean by that?

CARNOUSTIE. What I mean is—can ye no' give him credit for the very sensible thing he did on his own initiative?

ALBERT (*worried*) Carnoustie!

EMMA (*flaring up*) Sensible thing!

CARNOUSTIE (*placidly*) His going out was most sensible.

EMMA (*almost shrieking*) After I'd told him not to?

CARNOUSTIE. Aye, that's what made it sensible.

EMMA. You . . .

CARNOUSTIE (*with a step towards Emma*) But I'll allow that his gettin' a wee bit tipsy—though very natural in the circumstances —wasna sensible. (*He looks at the broken vases on the floor*) No, that was deplorable.

(DAPHNE *enters* R)

EMMA. If anyone had told me that I would ever stand and listen to such downright impudence . . .

CARNOUSTIE. And if anyone had told me that I would ever see a wife treating her husband as if he was a . . . (*He pauses briefly as his mind is called to more urgent matters*) Excuse me. (*To Albert*) Albert, it's out in the yard, isn't it? (*He moves to the door* R)

(DAPHNE *looks at Carnoustie with eyes filled with admiration*)

(*To Daphne*) Excuse me.

(CARNOUSTIE *exits* R)

EMMA (*having recovered her breath*) That young man leaves here as soon as the wedding's over, doesn't he? And the sooner the better. And I can't say much for your choice of friends. (*She moves down L of the table*)

ALBERT (*moving below the table*) Look, Ma. We're all a bit on edge tonight, so the least said the better. If you don't mind, I'll just see Shirley for a few minutes; then Carnoustie and me'll be getting off next door.

EMMA. You're not going next door.

ALBERT. Not going?

EMMA. We've had to make other arrangements. You'll both have to sleep on this thing.

ALBERT (*dismayed*) Oh. If we'd known we could have stayed the night at Toddy's place.

EMMA. Who's Toddy? One of your drinking friends, I suppose?

ALBERT. Well—yes.

EMMA. Then you're safer here. But I'll tell you what you can do. You can get yourself round to Toddy's place—as you call it —first thing in the morning, and stay there till it's time to go to the church. We don't want to run the risk of you seeing Shirley before the wedding. And if that doesn't suit—you can make your *own* arrangements. There's blankets and sheets over there. You can make up your own bed, I hope?

ALBERT. Yes, thanks.

EMMA (*turning to Henry*) Henry!

(HENRY *leaps up with a wail*)

HENRY. Yes, Emma. (*He sits again*)

EMMA. Get to bed.

HENRY (*weakly*) Yes, Emma. (*He rises and moves up* C) I think I'll just go and say good night to my ferrets.

EMMA (*this is the last straw*) You'll do no such thing—you drunken old reprobate . . .

(EMMA *takes* HENRY *by the scruff of the neck and propels him off* L. HENRY *is shot through the doorway, then* EMMA *follows him off.* ALBERT *looks towards the door* L, *lost in thought, and not happy thought. After a moment,* DAPHNE *moves to Albert*)

DAPHNE (*quietly*) Shall I give you a hand?

ALBERT (*coming to*) M'mm?

DAPHNE (*crossing to* R *of the bed*) To make up the bed.

ALBERT. No, no. We can manage. Thanks all the same.

DAPHNE. It's no trouble.

ALBERT (*crossing to* L *of the bed*) Trouble! I seem to have caused nothing but trouble ever since I got here.

DAPHNE (*gently*) Don't you believe it, Albert. (*She picks up a sheet*) You're not the cause of the trouble. You're only the excuse for it.

(DAPHNE *unfolds the sheet and they spread it on the bed*)

ALBERT. But I—I don't know what I've done. Oh, I know I went out when Shirl told me not to. Perhaps I shouldn't have done—I dunno. But even before that—the minute I got here, in fact—Ma was picking on me.

(DAPHNE *gets the second sheet and unfolds it*)

DAPHNE. Of course she was.

(*They spread the second sheet*)

Good Lord, you've met her sort before, haven't you? There are plenty of them about. That's how they get their happiness— making everybody's life a hell.

ALBERT (*incredulously*) You mean to say, she *likes* being the way she is?

(*They tuck in the sheets*)

DAPHNE. I should think she does. She wallows in it. (*She gets the blanket and spreads it*)

ALBERT. Good Lord! (*He stands agape, holding the edge of the blanket*)

DAPHNE (*practically*) Tuck your end in. (*She tucks in the blanket*) And, of course, some husbands *like* their wives like that.

ALBERT. You're not telling me that—Pop's one of those?

DAPHNE. No. All Uncle Henry has ever asked out of life is— his fair share of peace, his bit of home comfort, and his ferrets— (*she pauses briefly*) and all he's got is—his ferrets. (*She moves up L*)

(CARNOUSTIE *enters* R, *removes his cap and puts it on the sideboard.* ALBERT *tucks in the blanket*)

(*She looks around*) There doesn't seem to be any pillows. I'll ask Shirley where I can find some.

ALBERT. No, no. We can manage. (*To Carnoustie*) Can't we, son?

DAPHNE (*laughing*) I like the way you call him "son". (*To Carnoustie*) You're old enough to be his grandfather, aren't you, Scottie?

CARNOUSTIE (*moving to* R *of the table*) No' in years, I'm no'.

DAPHNE (*moving up* L *of the table; trying to imitate the accent*) I didna mean in years. Mon! I was proud of ye; the way ye stood up to Aunt Emma just now. Ma hairt fair warmed to ye.

CARNOUSTIE. I'd like to know what clan ye think ye belong to with an accent like that?

DAPHNE (*to Albert*) Isn't he sweet?

(ALBERT *folds the top of the sheet and blanket down*)

CARNOUSTIE. What for why are ye makin' up the bed? Are we no' going next door?

DAPHNE. No, you're not.

(ALBERT *moves to* L *of the bed and spreads the eiderdown on it*)

CARNOUSTIE (*to Daphne*) You mean we're sleeping here?

DAPHNE. We! (*She moves towards Carnoustie*) Thanks for the invitation.

CARNOUSTIE (*backing to the fireplace*) Oh, here now!

(EDIE *enters nervously* R)

EDIE (*looking around*) Is it all right?

DAPHNE (*drawing Edie up* R) Come in, Aunt Edie. The coast's clear now. "The fight is o'er, the battle lost." (*She puts an arm around Edie and takes her up* C) Poor Aunt Edie. Shut herself in the pantry, didn't you, darling?

EDIE. It was silly of me; but you know your Aunt Emma frightens me sometimes. (*She points to the bed*) Will you boys be all right on that thing? (*She moves to* R *of the bed*)

ALBERT. We'll be fine, thanks, Aunt Edie.

EDIE. Oh, but you haven't got any pillows. (*She moves up* LC) I must go and . . .

ALBERT (*intercepting Edie above the bed*) What you must do is stop worrying about—well, stop worrying, see? (*He puts his arm around her*)

EDIE (*suddenly bursting into tears and burying her face on Albert's breast*) Oh, Albert! I do want you and Shirley to be happy. You will be—won't you?

ALBERT (*comforting her*) 'Course we will, Aunt Edie. Once I've finished my service and we get settled down in Badcaster—away from—away from here.

(EDIE *looks up at Albert in wonder*)

And you must come over and see us sometimes. Promise?

EDIE (*bewildered*) But what about . . .? Aren't you going to live at Number Twenty-Four, then?

ALBERT. Number Twenty-Four? Twenty-Four what—where?

(CARNOUSTIE *moves to* R *of the table*)

EDIE (*still bewildered*) I thought Emma had . . .

ALBERT (*very much on the alert*) You thought she'd what? What are you talking about, Aunt Edie?

EDIE (*distressed*) Oh, dear! Now what have I done? I just took it for granted you'd know; that Shirley would have told you.

ALBERT (*almost impatiently*) Told me *what*?

EDIE. Albert, I—I'd rather not—I don't want to cause any more trouble. (*She turns to exit* L)

(ALBERT *suddenly picks Edie up and puts her on to the bed, in a sitting-up position, and puts the eiderdown round her*)

ALBERT. Now wait a minute, Aunt Edie. You're not moving out of that bed until you've told me what the devil you're talking about.

DAPHNE (*moving up* L *of the table*) You keep quiet, Aunt Edie, and you'll have the night of your life.

CARNOUSTIE (*with a glare of disapproval*) Tut-tut. (*He turns to the fireplace*)

(DAPHNE *looks at Carnoustie*)

ALBERT (*sitting on the right arm of the bed*) Come on, Aunt Edie, out with it.

(CARNOUSTIE *turns*)

EDIE (*sitting like a little bird in the bed*) Oh, dear! Well, Albert, I—I can only think that Shirley was going to tell you tomorrow as a—a—(*she tries to believe this*) wonderful surprise. You see—Number Twenty-Four—three doors up this street—was suddenly put up for sale, privately, about a fortnight ago it was, and—well—Emma—so kindly—as your wedding present—put down the deposit with the Building Society, so that you and Shirley could buy the house. (*She pauses*) That's all.

(ALBERT *rises slowly. The others watch him intently*)

ALBERT (*crossing slowly to the fireplace*) That's all.

(*There is a long silence.* CARNOUSTIE *moves up* C *and stands with his back to the audience*)

EDIE (*at last; apprehensively*) Can I get up now? (*She gets out of the bed, straightens it and crosses to* L *of Albert*) You won't say anything to Shirley or Emma—that I told you, I mean?

(DAPHNE *moves to* L *of the table.* CARNOUSTIE *turns and leans on the sideboard*)

ALBERT. Bless you, of course I won't. (*He kisses her*)
EDIE. Shirley's sure to tell you herself. Good night, Albert.
ALBERT. Good night, Aunt Edie. (*He kisses Edie and turns to the fireplace*) Sleep tight.

(EDIE *gives Albert a little squeeze, then moves to Carnoustie and holds out her hand*)

EDIE. Good night.

(CARNOUSTIE *unexpectedly kisses Edie.* DAPHNE'S *eyes open wide*)
CARNOUSTIE. Guid nicht.

(EDIE *crosses and exits* L)

DAPHNE. Well, of course . . . (*She rubs her hands together, and the look in her eyes suggests that, having seen Edie's technique, she is going to use it, too. She is not unmindful of Albert's dejection; therefore she overplays a little, in order to try to lighten the darkness. She crosses to Albert*) Good night, Albert. (*She gives just the slightest tilt of the chin, for a kiss*)

ALBERT (*automatically*) Good night, Daphne. Sleep tight. (*He kisses her*)

(DAPHNE *turns, looks at Carnoustie, then following Edie's technique, she approaches him with her hand out*)

DAPHNE. Good night, Scottie.

(CARNOUSTIE, *to* DAPHNE's *dismay, takes her hand, very much at arm's length, and shakes it*)

CARNOUSTIE (*briefly*) Ay. Guid nicht.

DAPHNE. Well, aren't you just a great big lump of Scotch Broth.

(DAPHNE *crosses and exits* L. CARNOUSTIE *picks up his case, puts it on the table, opens it and takes out a towel and sponge bag*)

CARNOUSTIE. Och! (*He takes a parcel from his case*) I'd forgotten all about this. (*He turns, parcel in hand; it is obviously his wedding present, but Albert is still turned away. He makes as if to give the parcel to Albert, stops, looks at him, then at the parcel, pauses, then quietly replaces the parcel in his case. Quietly*) I'll away to the back kitchen for a wash. (*He picks up his towel and sponge bag and moves to the door* R)

ALBERT (*turning*) What? Oh, yes. I suppose I'd better . . .

(CARNOUSTIE *exits* R)

(*Suddenly*) Oh, what the hell! (*He crosses to the chair* L, *removes his lanyard and silk, puts them on the chair, then goes to the table* C *and empties his pocket of cigarettes, matches and handkerchief and puts them on the table. He moves down* C, *faces* R *and struggles to remove his tight uniform jumper*)

(*Just as* ALBERT *has got his jumper over his head and covering his face, the door* L *opens.*

SHIRLEY *enters* L, *and comes nervously into the room. She is in pyjamas and dressing-gown*)

SHIRLEY. Oh. Is—is that you, Albert? (*She moves* C *and tries to recognize him*)

ALBERT (*struggling*) What? Is that you, Shirl? (*He turns to face her*)

SHIRLEY. Yes, Albert.

ALBERT. I'll be with you in a minute. (*He struggles*)

(SHIRLEY *takes a hand, and eventually* ALBERT *emerges from the jumper*)

(*He sees Shirley*) Hello!

SHIRLEY. Hello! Where's Carnoustie? (*She puts the jumper on the chair* L *of the table*)

ALBERT. He's out in the back kitchen, washing. (*He sits on the downstage end of the bed and holds out his hand to Shirley*)

(SHIRLEY *sits on* ALBERT's *knee and snuggles up to him for a while*)

SHIRLEY (*presently*) Did you think I wasn't coming down to see you?

ALBERT. I hoped you would.

SHIRLEY. You don't deserve it, really, not after what you did tonight.

(ALBERT *looks enquiringly at Shirley*)

Oh, Albert, *why* did you do it?

ALBERT. Do what?

SHIRLEY. It was bad enough *you* going out after I'd asked you not to; but to persuade dad to follow you, and to get him *drunk* into the bargain . . . Albert, did you do it deliberately—to annoy mum?

ALBERT (*quietly*) No—I didn't.

SHIRLEY. You don't like mum very much, do you?

ALBERT. She's never given me much cause to, has she?

SHIRLEY. Well—she doesn't *know* you very well, does she? I mean, she hasn't seen a great deal of you, has she?

ALBERT. Neither have you, for that matter.

SHIRLEY. No, but—that's different. I love you.

ALBERT (*with great tenderness*) Shirl. (*He kisses her*)

SHIRLEY (*laughing*) Now then, Albert Tufnell. There'll be plenty of time for that—(*she smiles demurely*) tomorrow. (*She ruffles his hair*) Are you scared about tomorrow, Albert?

ALBERT (*after a pause*) Tomorrow? It isn't tomorrow I'm worried about.

SHIRLEY. Worried? Are you worried? What about? Mum?

(ALBERT *does not reply*)

You needn't be. She isn't always like she's been tonight.

ALBERT (*with his eyes wide open; it almost bursts from him*) Good Lord, I should hope not! And a fat lot of consolation *that* is!

SHIRLEY (*nettled*) Well, after all, she did have some cause, didn't she? She's got all the worry of the wedding on her mind. Then, on top of that, you had to go and get dad drunk . . .

ALBERT. I . . .! Shirl, what makes you so sure I got your dad drunk? As a matter of fact he didn't come into the bar we were in until just before we left. We could tell he'd had a few—so we didn't even ask him to have *one*. We just brought him straight home.

SHIRLEY. You mean, he'd been drinking on his own?

ALBERT. Yes, he had.

SHIRLEY. But why? If he'd sneaked out to join you, why didn't he?

ALBERT (*quietly*) He told me why. He said he felt ruddy miserable; he didn't want to spoil our party. So he had a few quick ones to cheer himself up.

SHIRLEY. Well, I hope you don't have to cheer yourself that way when we're married.

ALBERT. I hope you'll never give me cause to.

SHIRLEY. I won't, Albert.

ALBERT. So long as we can be on our own, Shirl, after we're married—for the first few years at any rate—till we've got—used to each other—so long as we can get away from—the family.

SHIRLEY. You mean, from mum, don't you?

ALBERT. Well, yes—I do. (*Directly*) And we're going to, aren't we?

(SHIRLEY *is now very uneasy, but tries to hide the fact*)

SHIRLEY. But, Albert, we—we can't go very far away, can we? I mean—you're going to this job you've been offered at Badcaster, and—Badcaster's only four miles away from here.

ALBERT (*after a longish look at her*) That's right. Those four miles will serve their purpose very nicely. Shirley, don't you see —(*he pauses briefly*) a place of our own, even if it's only a couple of rooms, in Badcaster—darling, don't you *see* how wonderful it will be?

SHIRLEY. But, Albert . . .

(CARNOUSTIE *enters* R. *He is divested of his jumper, which he carries over his arm*)

CARNOUSTIE (*surprised at seeing Shirley*) Oh! Oh!

(CARNOUSTIE *exits* R)

ALBERT. But what, Shirl?

(SHIRLEY *looks away from him, then rises nervously and moves down* R *of the table*)

(*Slowly*) What were you going to say to me?

SHIRLEY (*after a slight pause*) Say? I—I can't—remember what it was.

ALBERT (*after a slight pause*) In that case it can't have been important, can it?

SHIRLEY (*gulping*) No.

(*There is a longish, awkward pause*)

(*Presently*) Well—I suppose I'd better get off to bed.

(ALBERT *rises.* SHIRLEY *moves up* R *of the table and crosses above it.* ALBERT *moves up* LC *and intercepts her*)

Daphne will be asleep, almost. I don't want to disturb her. (*She tries to smile*) And there's poor Carnoustie in the back kitchen. (*She moves close to Albert*) Good night, my darling. (*She kisses him passionately*) Tell me you love me.

ALBERT (*holding her tightly to him*) I love you, Shirl.

SHIRLEY. Tell me you'll always love me. No matter, if . . . (*She breaks off*)

ALBERT (*after waiting for her to go on*) If what?

SHIRLEY (*in a smothered voice*) Just tell me you'll always love me.
ALBERT (*quietly*) I'll always love you.

(SHIRLEY *hugs him, then crosses to the door* L)

(*Quite lightly*) Shirley, I wish you'd tell me something.
SHIRLEY (*with just a little start*) What?
ALBERT (*after a pause; facing her*) Whatever's in your mind.
SHIRLEY (*moving to* L *of him*) I love you, Albert Tufnell—and I always will. (*She gives him a short kiss and steps back*) There!
ALBERT (*after a pause*) You've nothing more to tell me?
SHIRLEY (*after a slight pause*) Isn't that enough?
ALBERT (*after a pause*) Yes, I suppose it'll have to be.
SHIRLEY (*in a whisper*) Good night.
ALBERT (*after the slightest pause*) Good night—my dear.

(SHIRLEY *exits* L. ALBERT *collects his jumper, puts it on the back of the chair* L, *then removes his collar and puts it on the chair* L.

CARNOUSTIE *enters* R. *He carries his jumper, silk, lanyard, towel and sponge bag. He puts the towel and bag in his case, the jumper over the back of the chair* L *of the table, and his silk and lanyard on the table. He then goes to the window, makes sure the curtains are closed, opens the door* L, *glances off, closes the door and moves above the right end of the bed. He is about to remove his trousers, but pauses a moment*)

CARNOUSTIE. Albert.
ALBERT. Yes? (*He moves to his case up* C)
CARNOUSTIE. D'think we're likely to have any more visitors?
ALBERT. Eh? I shouldn't think so. Lock the door if you're . . .
(*He takes his towel and sponge bag from his case*)
CARNOUSTIE. Och, there's no key. I've just looked. (*He slips off his trousers, folds them neatly and puts them on the chair* L *of the table*)
ALBERT. I suppose I'd better go and wash.
CARNOUSTIE (*now only in his shirt*) Ay, I should.

(ALBERT *exits* R, *leaving the door open*)

(*He moves to the bed, tests the springs, then contemplates the bed as a whole*) It's a queer bloody contraption, this. (*He rolls up his money-belt, places it under the mattress, removes his shoes and socks, then collects the two kitbags from the window alcove. He calls*) Albert.
ALBERT (*off; calling*) Yes?
CARNOUSTIE. Which side of the bed do you sleep?
ALBERT (*off*) I'm not fussy.
CARNOUSTIE. You can sleep on the left.
ALBERT (*off*) O.K.
CARNOUSTIE. If ye sleep at a'. (*He puts his kitbag on the right side of the bed as a pillow and Albert's kitbag as a pillow on the left side. He gets into bed, lies down, hits his head on something hard in his kitbag and reacts. He sits up, rubbing his head. He then knocks on his kitbag in several places. The bag would appear to be filled with blocks of wood.*

Finally he knocks on Albert's bag; it is much softer. He changes kitbags, then lies back in comfort, his legs diagonally across the bed)

(ALBERT *enters* R. *He has removed his trousers and has them over his arm. He puts his towel and sponge bag in his case, lays his trousers over the case, then moves to* L *of the table)*

(*With his face buried in bedclothes*) It's no' sae bad when you get used to it.

ALBERT (*misunderstanding*) How do you know? You've never even tried it.

CARNOUSTIE (*emerging from the bedclothes and sitting up*) What the hell are ye talkin' aboot?

ALBERT. Married life, of course.

CARNOUSTIE. Och, I was talking aboot this bed.

ALBERT. Oh? Sorry. (*He takes two cigarettes from his pocket and lights one*)

CARNOUSTIE. Och, ye need not apologize. It's only natural that the perilous step ye're aboot to take should be uppermost in your mind. Aye, ma God, it is.

ALBERT. H'mm! (*He moves to* R *of the bed*) Fag? (*He hands the lighted cigarette to Carnoustie and lights the other one for himself*)

CARNOUSTIE. Ay. Ta. Ye know, it's a disgustin' habit, smoking in bed; but I ha'e na doot your wee wifie will cure ye of it.

(ALBERT *collects his trousers, crosses to the chair* L, *puts the trousers on it, then, only in his shirt, shoes and socks, starts to get into bed. He remembers his shoes and socks and removes them.* CARNOUSTIE *uses his shoe as an ashtray*)

ALBERT (*about to get into bed*) Oi!

CARNOUSTIE. Hello?

ALBERT. Move over.

CARNOUSTIE. Sorry. (*He moves over a little*)

(ALBERT *gets into bed. Both pull the bedclothes up simultaneously. Both smoke simultaneously*)

(*After a pause*) Albert.

ALBERT. Yes?

CARNOUSTIE (*solemnly*) I've no wish to appear presumptuous, and to interfere in your married life, but—I don't want . . .

ALBERT (*almost eagerly*) Go on.

CARNOUSTIE. I'd like to gi'e ye a wee worrd of advice.

ALBERT. Yes?

CARNOUSTIE (*solemnly*) Tomorrow—before ye set oot on your honeymoon, I think it's essential ye should——

ALBERT. What?

CARNOUSTIE. —buy yoursel' a suit of pyjamas.

ALBERT (*not expecting this, of course*) Oh! (*He pauses*) You do?

CARNOUSTIE. Aye. (*He pauses*) If only for the look of the thing.

ALBERT (*after a pause*) I'll slip out in the morning and get some.

CARNOUSTIE. I *should.*
ALBERT. I will. (*He pauses*) Thanks for telling me.
CARNOUSTIE. Not at a'.

(*They smoke in silence*)

(*Presently*) Ye'll drop me a line and let me know how ye're getting on—on your honeymoon?
ALBERT. I will.
CARNOUSTIE (*after a slight pause*) Just a general outline. No details.

(*They smoke in silence*)

ALBERT (*presently*) I expect you'll be thinking about me.
CARNOUSTIE. I hope to keep ma imagination well under control.

(*They smoke in silence*)

ALBERT (*presently*) Carnoustie.
CARNOUSTIE. Ay?
ALBERT. Shirley hasn't said anything.
CARNOUSTIE. What aboot?
ALBERT. Buying that house.
CARNOUSTIE. Oh, did she no'?
ALBERT. No. (*He pauses*) I wish she had.
CARNOUSTIE. Aye. I see wha' ye mean. It presents a problem, that does.
ALBERT. There's an awful lot of problems presented themselves, if you ask me.
CARNOUSTIE. Aye. (*He nips out his cigarette and puts the stub very carefully on the floor*) Still, Albert, d'ye know the best way tae deal wi' problems?
ALBERT. No?
CARNOUSTIE. Sleep on 'em. (*He slides down into the bed*)
ALBERT. I think you're right. (*He stubs out his cigarette and slides down into the bed*)

(CARNOUSTIE *has the lion's share of the bedclothes.* ALBERT *drags over his fair share. He lies down, bangs his head on the kitbag, reacts, throws out the bag over the head of the bed and takes half of the other bag for his pillow. Both stretch their legs and their feet emerge at the foot of the bed. There is a pause*)

(*Only the top of his head is visible*) Carnoustie.
CARNOUSTIE (*only the top of his head is visible*) Aye?
ALBERT. The light.
CARNOUSTIE. Wha' aboot it?
ALBERT. It's on.
CARNOUSTIE. Well, put it oot.
ALBERT (*after a tiny pause*) The switch is on your side.

(CARNOUSTIE *stirs, grunts, gets out of bed, moves towards the door* R, *realizes the switch is by the door* L *and turns*)

CARNOUSTIE. You're a horrible man. (*He crosses towards the door* L)

EDIE *enters* L. *She carries two pillows. She lets out a scream as her eyes fall on Carnoustie, and buries her face in the pillows.* CARNOUSTIE, *with a yell, takes a flying leap at the bed and lands on top of Albert. For a second there is confusion, at the end of which* ALBERT *is on the floor on one side of the bed and* CARNOUSTIE *is on the floor on the other side.*

VERY QUICK CURTAIN

SCENE 2

SCENE—*The same. Ten forty-five the next morning.*

When the CURTAIN *rises, the bed is folded away and the room tidy.* CARNOUSTIE *is standing at the mirror down* R, *finishing tidying himself up for the wedding and combing his hair. Henry's jacket is on the back of the armchair.* DAPHNE, *in her bridesmaid's clothes, enters* L *and moves down* LC.

DAPHNE (*with a smile*) Will I do?

(CARNOUSTIE *turns and looks at Daphne*)

CARNOUSTIE (*deeply*) Ay. Ye wud that.

DAPHNE (*crossing to Carnoustie and adjusting his wedding ribbon*) I expect you're congratulating yourself you're not in Albert's place.

CARNOUSTIE. I'm no' complaining o' ma ain position at the moment. (*He turns towards the mirror, but finding Daphne in the way, he indicates the settee*) Will ye no' like to sit down?

DAPHNE. That's the second time you've asked me to share *that* with you.

CARNOUSTIE (*shocked*) Ohh! I wasna' going to . . .

DAPHNE (*crossing and sitting on the settee*) Come on. (*She pats the seat beside her*)

CARNOUSTIE. I doot if there'll be time.

DAPHNE (*quickly*) Time for what?

(CARNOUSTIE *crosses and sits* R *of Daphne on the settee, but leaves a space between them*)

CARNOUSTIE (*sternly*) For sitting doon. Ha'e I no' to be awa' in a couple o' moments to pick up the bridegroom?

DAPHNE. Still, it's wonderful what can be done in a couple of moments, isn't it?

CARNOUSTIE. I'm no' a quick worker.

DAPHNE. I expect you make a good job of it once you start. Have you kissed the bride, yet? (*She moves close to him*)

CARNOUSTIE. My goodness, no. (*He edges away to the right end of the settee*)

DAPHNE. You have to—after the wedding—you know. And— then there's the best man's privilege.

CARNOUSTIE. What's that?

DAPHNE. You can kiss anyone else you like. (*She moves closer to him*)

CARNOUSTIE (*lured to her but pulling himself back*) I'm no' a kisser. (*He looks away from her*)

DAPHNE. You've got to begin sometime. *And* with someone. (*She puts her face up to his*)

(CARNOUSTIE *turns to Daphne, finds they are nose to nose and rises hastily*)

CARNOUSTIE. It's time I wasn't here.

DAPHNE. What are we going to do after the wedding, Carnoustie?

CARNOUSTIE (*straightening his collar; taken aback*) Do? Who? (*He moves up* C)

DAPHNE. You and me.

CARNOUSTIE. I hadna' given the matter much consideration. Are we supposed to do something?

DAPHNE (*looking tentatively at him*) Of course, there's always the pictures. (*She rises, moves to the chair* L *of the table and puts one knee on it*)

CARNOUSTIE. Well, now, I . . .

DAPHNE. I've got an idea. (*She sits* L *of the table*) You know, I owe you half a crown. (*With a smile*) I hadn't forgotten.

CARNOUSTIE. No, neither had I.

DAPHNE. Well—*I'll* pay for your seat with that; and *you* can pay for mine.

CARNOUSTIE (*moving above Daphne; in admiration*) Daphne— girl, you should have been born a Scotswoman.

DAPHNE. If I had, I'd have made you pay for both of us.

CARNOUSTIE. But that's . . .

(EMMA *enters* L. *Her hair is in a net. This apart, she is dressed for the wedding. She carries a smartish handbag. Throughout the entire scene she gives the impression that she is fighting a losing battle against time, fat, and other malignant forces. It may be a losing battle, but it is certainly a speedy one*)

EMMA (*as she bustles in*) Now then! Now then! What are you two doing?

(CARNOUSTIE *moves to* L *of the sideboard*)

DAPHNE. Nothing, Aunt Emma. Everything's done, isn't it?

(EMMA *crosses to the sideboard and takes an old black handbag from the cupboard*)

EMMA. That's what *you* think! I thought you were supposed to be helping Shirley to dress?

DAPHNE. I was, but—well, you came in and—took over, didn't you?

EMMA (*moving above the table* c) Yes, and you can go and take over again from where I left off. (*She transfers articles from the old bag to the new*) Off you go.

DAPHNE (*rising*) Yes, Aunt Emma.

(DAPHNE *exits* L)

EMMA (*calling after Daphne*) And if she wants *me*, tell her she can't have me. I'm going to the wedding as well as her. (*To Carnoustie*) Isn't it about time *you* were getting off?

CARNOUSTIE. It's no' so very far from here to Toddy's.

EMMA. Has Albert arranged for the taxi to pick you both up at this Toddy's place?

CARNOUSTIE. Yes, he has.

EMMA. And will Toddy, as you call him, be coming to the Church?

CARNOUSTIE. Aye, I expect he'll want to see Albert going through the hoop.

EMMA. What?

CARNOUSTIE. I mean, getting married.

EMMA (*replacing the old bag in the sideboard cupboard*) H'm! Well, if he wants to—(*big-hearted Emma*) you can tell him he can come to the reception, afterwards.

CARNOUSTIE. Thank you very much.

EMMA (*with sudden alarm*) Oh, the ring. Did Albert give you the ring before he went?

(*The following six lines are taken at terrific speed*)

CARNOUSTIE. Aye, he did.

EMMA. Have you got it put away safe?

CARNOUSTIE. I have.

EMMA. Where is it?

CARNOUSTIE. In ma pocket.

EMMA. Let me see it. Let me see it.

(CARNOUSTIE *produces the ring.* EMMA *takes it from him, peers at it and rubs it on her dress*)

(*She calls*) Edie, fetch me the rag I polish the brass with. (*She breathes on the ring and rubs it once or twice on her sleeve*) I suppose it *is* gold.

(EDIE *enters* R *and crosses to* R *of Emma. She is without her hat and coat. She carries a duster*)

EDIE (*as she enters*) Here we are, Emma.
EMMA. Thank you.

(EDIE *holds out the duster and sees the ring*)

EDIE (*pointing to the ring*) Ooh! Is that Shirley's? (*She gulps*)
EMMA. It is. Such as it is. (*She takes the duster, but lets Edie have a long look at the ring*)
EDIE (*in a choking voice*) Oh, Emma, isn't it beautiful—isn't it beauti—— (*Again memories are blessing and burning*)

(EDIE *can only gurgle, wag her head, dab her eyes and rush off* R)

EMMA (*polishing the ring and nodding her head after Edie*) Of course, she's going to have the time of her life.

(*The front-door bell rings*)

CARNOUSTIE. Shall I answer the door, Mrs Hornett?
EMMA (*with great resignation*) No, I'll go. (*She puts the duster and ring on the table* C *and goes to the door* L) If I get to the wedding *at all*, at this rate, I'll be lucky.

(EMMA *exits* L)

CARNOUSTIE (*to himself*) And if you *don't*—everybody else will. (*He picks up the ring and looks at it*) My puir Albert. (*He pockets the ring*)
EMMA (*off; calling*) Shirley.
SHIRLEY (*off upstairs; calling*) Yes, Mum?
EMMA (*off*) Bouquets have come.

(EMMA *enters* L. *She carries a cellophane bag containing the bridal bouquet, two bridesmaid's posies and three carnation buttonholes*)

(*As she enters*) I began to think these were never coming. (*She takes out the flowers*) Oh—very nice.
CARNOUSTIE. Aye—they're bonnie.
EMMA (*handing two buttonholes to Carnoustie*) Here! One for Albert and one for you.
CARNOUSTIE. But, just a minute, Mrs Hornett . . .
EMMA. Never mind "Mrs Hornetting". Put yours in now. (*She snatches one buttonhole from him*) Here! I'll do it. (*She runs her hand down the right side of his collar*) Hah! No buttonhole—I'll have to get you a pin. (*She moves towards the sideboard*)
CARNOUSTIE. But, Mrs Hornett! Albert and I canna wear these things.
EMMA. Why, what's the matter with them?
CARNOUSTIE. There's nothing the matter with them—it's no' that.
EMMA. Then who says you can't?
CARNOUSTIE (*almost shouting*) Her Majesty the Queen.
EMMA. What!

CARNOUSTIE. It's against regulations. We'd be hanged, drawn and quartered if Her Majesty saw us wearing flowers on our uniform.

EMMA (*defeated*) H'mmm! (*With a sniff*) Didn't know Albert had invited *Royalty* to his wedding. (*She takes the other buttonhole from him*) Well, that's another two three-and-sixes gone down the drain, as well as Rita's posy. (*She puts one buttonhole on the table and holds up the other*) Henry had better wear one of these. Where is he?

CARNOUSTIE. I think he's oot bye wi' his ferrets.

EMMA. Out with his ferrets! His only daughter's getting married in half an hour and all he can think about is . . . (*She moves to the door* R *and calls*) Edie. Tell Henry to come in here. I want him. (*She turns*) Ferrets!

CARNOUSTIE. Well, I suppose I may as well be getting off, now. (*He collects his cap from the sideboard*) There's nothing more for me to do, is there?

EMMA. No, there isn't. Off you go.

(CARNOUSTIE *moves towards the door* L)

(*She suddenly rushes to the table*) Oh, the ring! Where is it? Did you . . .?

CARNOUSTIE (*stopping and turning*) Aye, I did.

EMMA. Where is it?

CARNOUSTIE. In ma pocket.

EMMA. Let me see it.

CARNOUSTIE. I . . . (*He sighs and produces the ring*)

EMMA. Now put it away, safe. Now you know what you've got to do, don't you?

CARNOUSTIE (*pocketing the ring*) Yes, I do.

EMMA. Has Albert given you some money for all the paying out you'll have to do?

CARNOUSTIE. Aye.

EMMA. Right. Then off you go. (*She moves to the mirror down* R *and pins the buttonhole on herself*)

(CARNOUSTIE *turns to go*)

(*She has another thought*) Wait! And tell Albert to speak up in church.

CARNOUSTIE. Right.

EMMA. Tell him when he says "I will", I want to hear it.

CARNOUSTIE. Aye. (*He turns to go*)

(DAPHNE *enters* L *and almost collides with Carnoustie*)

DAPHNE. Oh! Isn't it time you were going?

CARNOUSTIE (*muttering with much feeling*) Aye, ma God, it is.

(CARNOUSTIE *exits* L)

DAPHNE (*moving above the table*) Shirley wants to know if she can see her bouquet, Aunt Emma.

EMMA. Can't she wait till she comes down?

DAPHNE. She says she wants to see it now.

EMMA. There it is.

(DAPHNE *picks up the bouquet*)

Mind how you carry it. Is she nearly ready?

DAPHNE (*moving up* LC) She's getting on.

(EDIE *enters* R. *She is a devil for punishment. She now wears her hat*)

EDIE (*as she enters*) I've told Henry, Emma, I . . . (*She sees the bouquet*) Ooooh! Is—is that Shirley's? (*She gulps*)

DAPHNE (*with justifiable apprehension*) Yes, Aunt Edie. Isn't it beautiful?

EDIE. Isn't it beautiful, Emma?

(EDIE *gurgles, wags her head, dabs her eyes and, punished, staggers off* R)

EMMA (*looking after Edie*) Well, if *I'm* not in a mental home by tonight, *she* will be.

DAPHNE. Poor Aunt Edie.

EMMA (*moving above the table*) "Poor Aunt Edie", nothing! (*She folds the cellophane bag*) She's stark, staring, raving mad. That's all that's the matter with *her*. Off you go. (*She indicates the bouquet*) Take that up to Shirley. Now where's Henry? I thought I told . . .

(HENRY *potters in* R. *He is in his shirt sleeves*)

DAPHNE. Here he is.

EMMA (*turning*) There you are.

HENRY (*not feeling too good*) Only just.

EMMA. And what do you mean by that?

HENRY. I'm not feeling too good. (*He indicates the bouquet*) Them for me?

(DAPHNE *giggles*)

EMMA (*ushering Daphne to the door; to Henry*) Well, you've only got yourself to blame.

(DAPHNE *exits* L)

If you will go out getting drunk . . .

HENRY. Edie says you wanted me.

EMMA. Yes, I do. It's high time you made yourself ready. (*She crosses to the armchair, picks up Henry's jacket and helps him into it*)

HENRY. But I've got to . . .

EMMA. You've got to do as I tell you. In case you've forgotten, you're giving your daughter away in holy matrimony in about five minutes' time.

HENRY. Wouldn't you want a bit of nourishment if *you'd* just given birth to six healthy young ferrets?

EMMA. 'Enry 'Ornett . . .!

HENRY. Rosie's got to have her milk.

EMMA (*with exasperation*) All right, then. Well go and give it to her and be quick about it.

(HENRY *turns to go*)

(*She picks up a buttonhole*) Wait. Here. (*She gets a pin from the mantel-piece and fastens the buttonhole to Henry's jacket*)

HENRY. Hey! It isn't me that's gettin' married.

EMMA (*muttering*) I wish it was—*and* to somebody else.

HENRY (*muttering*) Same 'ere.

EMMA. H'm! Encouraging you to throw your weight about a bit, isn't it—having Albert and Carnasty in the house. Never mind, we'll soon get you back in your place, my lad. (*She finishes with the buttonhole*) Off you go.

(HENRY *exits* R)

(*She calls*) And when you come in, give yourself a brush down and give your hands a good wash. We don't want you arriving at church smelling of ferrets. Edie!

EDIE (*off*) Yes, Emma?

(EDIE *enters* R. *She has her coat half on*)

EMMA. Are you nearly ready to get yourself off down to *Banfields?*

EDIE. Yes, Emma.

EMMA. You know what you've got to do, don't you?

EDIE. Yes, Emma.

EMMA. Good. Now I'm going upstairs to finish getting myself ready. (*She glances at the clock and crosses to the door* L) Yes, and I've about three minutes to do it in.

(EDIE *moves up* C)

Fine sight I'll look. Not that it matters what *I* look like. I'm only the bride's mother.

MRS LACK (*off* R; *calling*) Are you there, Emma?

EMMA. Oh, my . . .! Get her out of here before I come down.

(EMMA *exits hurriedly* L.

MRS LACK *enters* R. *She is dressed for the wedding in a highly-coloured dress and a rakish hat*)

MRS LACK (*as she enters*) It's only me. (*She sees Edie*) Oh, it's only you, Edie.

EDIE. Yes, it's only me. I thought you'd be on your way to church by now, Mrs Lack. How's poor Rita?

MRS LACK (*moving to the mirror down* R) Don't talk to me about poor Rita. (*She takes a compact from her handbag and powders her nose*) Carrying on something awful, she is, 'cos she isn't going to the wedding. (*She sits in the armchair*) I began to think I'd never get there myself. (*She replaces the compact in her bag*) Doctor's only just gone. (*She scratches her arm, then realizes what she is doing*) 'Scuse me, but seeing all them spots on Rita . . . Emma hasn't gone yet, has she? I wanted to ask her if she'd mind giving me a lift to the church—everything throwing me so late.

EDIE. You'll have to ask her, won't you?

(*The toot of a taxi horn is heard off*)

(*In a panic*) Oh, is that the taxi? (*She gallops to the window and peers out*) Yes, it is. I must tell Emma. (*She runs to the door* L) Lovely white ribbons on it.

(EDIE *exits* L)

(*Off; calling*) Emma! The taxi! The taxi's come! Daphne!

(EDIE *re-enters* L, *panting*)

I've told them. (*She gallops to the window*)

(*The front-door bell rings.*
   EDIE *exits* L *and opens the front door*)

(*Off*) They'll be down in a minute, now, driver. (*She calls*) Emma!

EMMA (*off*) All right! All right! Have you got rid of that woman, yet?

(MRS LACK *reacts and rises*)

EDIE (*off*) She says she wants to know whether she can ride down to the church with you.

(EDIE *enters* L)

Oh, dear! I'd better tell Henry.

(EDIE *crosses and exits* R)

(*Off; calling*) Henry! The taxi's come. Emma's just going.
HENRY (*off*) Good.
EDIE (*off*) I think you'd better come in, Henry.

(EDIE *enters* R, *panting*)

Oh, dear! Oh, dear! (*She moves down* R)

MRS LACK (*sorrowfully*) This must be bringing it all back to you, Edie.

(EDIE *gulps, wags and gurgles.*
HENRY *enters* R *and moves up* C)

Well, Mr 'Ornett. This must be a sad day for you. (*She moves to*
R *of Henry*)
HENRY. It is. Rosie's just lost one of her young ones.
EDIE (*with a step towards Henry*) Has it died?
HENRY. Yes, poor little thing. Look. (*Practically under Mrs
Lack's nose, he opens his hand and reveals a small bundle of fur, Rosie's
property, deceased*)
MRS LACK (*with a yelp*) Aaah! (*She recoils up* R)
EDIE (*alarmed*) Henry, you didn't ought to.

(EMMA, *now fully dressed, bustles in* L. HENRY *moves* RC)

If Emma saw you with that thing . . .
EMMA. With what thing? (*She moves above the table*) Where's my
bag? Ah, there it is. (*She picks up her bag*) Morning, Florrie.
Henry, go and get your hat. I want to see you wearing it before
I go. Go on, hurry.
HENRY. Aye. All right. (*He still has the baby ferret in his hand. He
does not know what to do with it, and wants to keep it out of Emma's
sight. The unfortunate Edie is standing by him. He turns furtively to her*)
Edie.
EDIE. Yes, Henry?
HENRY (*putting the ferret in Edie's hand*) Get rid of it, will you?

(HENRY *crosses and exits* L.

EDIE *looks down at the dead ferret and gives a little scream, but
loyalty to Henry prevents her from dropping it. Shuddering and almost
fainting, she dashes off* R)

EMMA (*looking after Edie*) She's up the pole. As God's my judge,
she's up the pole. (*To Mrs Lack*) Now what's this about you
wanting to ride down to the church with me?
MRS LACK. Well, if you don't mind, Emma. You see . . .
EMMA. Yes, I see! Well, I suppose you'll *have* to. (*She crosses to
the mirror*) Are you all ready, 'cos we are? (*She looks in the mirror
and adjusts her hat*)
MRS LACK. Yes, Emma. I'm all ready.

(DAPHNE *enters* L)

DAPHNE (*to Mrs Lack*) Oh, good morning.
MRS LACK (*moving above the table and looking at Daphne's dress*)
Oh, yes. You look very well. You make a nice bridesmaid, don't
you? But I wish you could have seen our Rita. *She* can wear that
colour. (*She moves below the sideboard*)

(EMMA *moves below the table, picks up a posy and hands it to
Daphne*)

EMMA. Here you are, Daphne.

DAPHNE. Thank you, Aunt Emma. Isn't it lovely! (*She moves down* L)

EMMA (*moving* RC) Lovely price, too.

(HENRY *enters* R *and stands up* C. *He wears a bowler hat*)

(*She moves to* R *of Henry*) Let me look at you. (*Doubtfully*) You'll do.

(SHIRLEY *enters* L. *She looks very charming in her wedding dress and is carrying her bouquet*)

MRS LACK (*with genuine delight*) Oh, Shirley, love! You look lovely.

SHIRLEY (*moving below the settee*) Thank you, Mrs Lack.

MRS LACK. Doesn't she look lovely, Emma?

EMMA. Well, even though she's my own daughter, I will say . . .

SHIRLEY. Thank you, Mum darling.

EMMA (*to Henry*) Well, 'aven't *you* got anything to say?

HENRY. Aye, when I get the chance. (*He moves to* R *of Shirley*) You look a real treat. Come on, give your old dad a kiss.

SHIRLEY (*avoiding him*) Dad, my make-up. (*She crosses to the mirror*)

HENRY (*disappointed*) Well, I will say one thing, you'll do Albert credit.

EMMA (*expostulating*) She'll do Albert credit! Well, I like that.

(*The sound of the taxi horn is heard off*)

Here! We'd better be off. Taxi's waiting. Now! Are we all ready? (*She calls*) Edie. (*She moves up* R)

EDIE (*off*) Yes, Emma?

(EDIE *dashes on* R, *her gloves in her hand. She stops dead as she sees Shirley. This is the last straw, so to speak. Deidre of the Sorrows has nothing on Edie at this moment*)

Oooh!

SHIRLEY. Do you like it, Aunt Edie? (*She pivots to display the dress*)

(EDIE *gulps, wags, gurgles, wrings her gloves and exits* R)

EMMA (*looking after Edie*) I mean to say! What *can* you do with her except put her in a strait jacket? (*She moves to* R *of the table*) Now, you'll be all right, won't you, Shirley love? You won't be nervous, will you? You've no need to be. I'm sure you look very nice. (*With surprising emotion for Emma*) You won't be my little girl any longer, will you? (*She actually sniffs once or twice*)

MRS LACK (*sententiously*) Never mind, Emma. You're losing a daughter, but gaining a son.

(EMMA *gives Mrs Lack a "thank you for nothing" look, then moves to* R *of Henry*)

EMMA. Now, Henry. Don't make a fool of yourself during the ceremony. (*She crosses towards the door* L) Oh—and don't start for the church for another five minutes. See you take Shirley down the aisle nicely. And while you're waiting, just you think out what you're going to say in your speech at the reception, and for goodness' sake, talk about your daughter; not about ferrets.

(*The taxi horn is heard off*)

(*She calls*) All right! We're coming! Daphne. Florrie. (*She bustles Daphne and Mrs Lack to the door* L) Got everything, Daphne? Now, Henry.

(DAPHNE *and* MRS LACK *exit* L)

(*She bustles to the door* R *and calls*) We're off, Edie. And don't forget, you go off to *Banfields* when Shirley and Henry go. And remember what I told you about them presents, and, Edie, do pull yourself together. We don't want you howling the place down and making everyone think they're at a funeral. (*She moves to Shirley and carefully kisses her*) Bye-bye, love. Bless you. (*She crosses to the door* L. *To Henry*) You give yourself a good brush down, it won't do any harm.

(EMMA *finally departs* L. SHIRLEY *and* HENRY *stand quite still for a moment after Emma's whirlwind speech and exit*)

HENRY (*presently*) Well, I'm glad we don't 'ave weddings every day.

SHIRLEY (*moving up* C) I'll get you the clothes brush, Dad. You *are* a bit dusty.

HENRY. Dusty!

SHIRLEY. Go into the back yard and give yourself a brush. (*She puts her bouquet on the table, takes a clothes brush from the sideboard drawer, gives the brush to Henry, then goes to the mirror down* R)

(EDIE *enters slowly and apprehensively* R. *She carries her handbag*)

HENRY (*grumbling*) I'll be glad when this is all over.

SHIRLEY. And put your buttonhole straight, Dad. It's a bit crooked.

(HENRY, *with something akin to a snarl, exits* R. EDIE, *whimpering a little, moves above the table and puts her handbag on it*)

You all right, Aunt Edie?

EDIE. I must be brave. I *will* be brave.

SHIRLEY. The taxi'll be here in a minute. It won't take them long. You're sure I look all right, Aunt Edie?

EDIE (*whimpering*) You look beautiful, love, beautiful. P'raps your veil's a bit crooked.

SHIRLEY (*rushing to the mirror; horrified*) What! It isn't, is it?

(*She fiddles with her veil*) Why didn't you tell me before? (*She turns*) Is that better?

EDIE. It's as straight as you'll get it. (*She moves to the fireplace*)

(SHIRLEY *crosses below the table to the window and peers out.*

HENRY *enters* R, *crosses and stands up* LC. *His buttonhole is now a few stalks and ends of fern*)

SHIRLEY (*turning*) The taxi—Dad, the taxi's here.

HENRY. I'm here! Now, come on. Let's get it over with. You ready, Shirley?

SHIRLEY. Do I look all right, Dad?

HENRY. Too late to do anything about it *now* if you don't. Come on.

(SHIRLEY, *after another doubtful whimper, gives a sudden yelp*)

SHIRLEY. *Dad!*

HENRY. What now?

EDIE (*moving up* R *of the table*) What is it?

SHIRLEY (*pointing in horror at Henry's buttonhole*) Your button-hole!

HENRY. What's wrong with it?

SHIRLEY. Well, *look* at it.

HENRY (*removing the remains of his buttonhole and looking at it*) Well, I'm damned! That's Rosie, that is.

SHIRLEY. *What!*

HENRY. When I went out just now she was in such a state at losing one of her young 'uns, I 'ad to pick 'er up and give her a little comfort, and she must 'ave nibbled the whole thing.

SHIRLEY (*nearly frantic*) For heaven's sake!

EDIE (*picking up a new buttonhole from the table*) Never mind, Shirley. There's another one here. (*She holds out the buttonhole to Shirley*)

(*The taxi horn sounds off*)

SHIRLEY (*snatching the buttonhole*) Come *on*, Dad. I'll have to fasten it in the taxi. We can't keep Albert and everyone waiting. Coming to see me off, Aunt Edie?

EDIE. Yes. (*She sobs*) No, it's no use, I can't.

(EDIE *dashes off* R)

SHIRLEY. Come on, Dad. Give me your arm.

HENRY. What for?

SHIRLEY (*with a howl of exasperation*) Oooh! Come on, Dad.

(SHIRLEY *crosses and exits* L.

HENRY *follows her off. The room is empty for a moment.*

EDIE *pokes her head round the door* R, *enters, moves to the table, picks up her handbag and sees Shirley's bouquet*)

C

EDIE (*picking up the bouquet*) Shirley! Your bouquet!

(EDIE, *with the bouquet in one hand and her bag in the other, dashes off* L. *The front door is heard to slam, then the taxi is heard driving away. There is a long pause, then the door* R *slowly opens.*

ALBERT *steps into the room. He stands still for a moment, as if listening to the silence, then he moves* C, *puts his cap on the table, picks up the remaining posy, smells it and puts it down. He crosses to the radio, switches it on, looks at the clock, takes out a cigarette, sits in the easy chair and lights the cigarette. The radio warms up, and a female voice is heard faintly singing. The song is "Early One Morning". The singing increases in volume as the song goes on*)

FEMALE VOICE (*through the radio; singing*)
    ". . . heard a maiden singing in the valley below,
      Oh, don't deceive me!
      Oh, never leave me!
    How could you treat a poor maiden so?"

        The CURTAIN *slowly falls*

ACT III

SCENE—*The same. About an hour later.*

When the CURTAIN *rises,* ALBERT *is pacing up and down the room, deep in troubled thought. A taxi is heard approaching.* ALBERT *moves quickly to the window and looks cautiously out. The taxi stops. The front door is heard to open, followed by a babel of voices,* EMMA'S *predominating.*

EMMA (*off*) Then—oh, my God! He'll pay for this! You just see if he doesn't. If I lay my hands on him, I'll kill him.

(ALBERT *grabs his hat and exits quickly* R, *slamming the door behind him.*

EMMA *enters* L, *leans for a moment on the table, then sits* L *of it*)

Oh, my God! Oh, my . . .! (*She passes her hand across her brow*) I can't believe it.

(*The taxi is heard to depart*)

(*She pulls herself together, rises and goes to the door* L) Henry! Shut that door.

(*The front door is heard to slam*)

We don't want the whole street poking their noses in to find out what's happened. Not that they don't know already, all of them. Daphne, bring Shirley in here. Come in here and lie down a bit, Shirley. (*She moves to the settee and arranges the cushions to serve as a pillow*)

(SHIRLEY, *almost supported by* DAPHNE, *enters slowly* L. SHIRLEY *is a pathetic sight. Her bouquet hangs limply down from one hand, her bridal veil is just a little askew, and she almost covers her face with her wisp of a handkerchief.* EMMA *helps* DAPHNE *bring* SHIRLEY *in*)

Come in here. Come and lie down.
SHIRLEY (*in tears*) Oh, Mum . . .

(DAPHNE *closes the door.* EMMA *helps* SHIRLEY *on to the settee*)

EMMA. There, there! You mustn't give in, love. Whatever happens, you mustn't give in. There we are. Put your feet up. (*She lifts Shirley's feet on to the settee*) That's better, isn't it? (*She adjusts the cushions*)

(SHIRLEY *lies back, with her head at the left end of the settee*)

SHIRLEY. Oh, Mum . . .

67

(DAPHNE *moves above the left end of the settee*)

EMMA (*moving above the right end of the settee*) Just lie back quiet, lie back and don't talk, and we'll get you a nice cup of tea.

SHIRLEY. I—I don't want a cup of tea. I just want to die.

EMMA (*not realizing quite what she is saying*) But you must have a cup of tea, first.

DAPHNE. Shall I go and make it, Aunt Emma?

EMMA. Yes, you can. You make some for all of us. Lord knows, I can do with one.

SHIRLEY (*wailing*) Oh, Daphne, what am I going to do? (*She sits up*)

DAPHNE (*putting her arm around Shirley*) Try not to think about it for a bit.

SHIRLEY. But—but . . . Oh, I can't help but think about it. I'll go mad, I know I will.

EMMA. Now, lie back and rest, same as I told you. Here, I'll take this off. (*She removes Shirley's veil*) And we'll take this off, too— (*she removes Shirley's coatee*) and you'll feel more comfortable.

SHIRLEY. Oooh! My veil! (*She weeps*)

EMMA (*taking the bouquet from Shirley*) And, Daphne, take this away. Put it somewhere out of sight, I never want to see it again.

(DAPHNE *takes the bouquet from Emma*)

SHIRLEY (*limply*) My bouquet!

(HENRY *enters slowly* L. *He looks dejected and apprehensive*)

EMMA (*moving and putting the veil and coatee on the sideboard; to Henry*) Oh, you've come in. You've been long enough, 'aven't you? You been talking to anybody?

HENRY (*crossing to the armchair*) No, I 'aven't. (*He removes his jacket, collar and tie, and puts them over the back of the armchair*)

EMMA (*moving to the cupboard up* L) Well, this is a nice mess, isn't it? (*She takes her slippers from the cupboard*)

HENRY. Aye, it is. (*He sits in the armchair, removes his boots, takes his slippers from the hearth and puts them on*)

EMMA. I never thought I'd live to see the day when a daughter of mine would . . .

SHIRLEY (*in tears*) Oh—Mum! (*Desperately*) I'm sure we should have waited at the church a bit longer. I'm sure he—would have —turned up. He might have had an accident. Something *must* have happened. He'd never . . . (*She sobs*)

EMMA. Go and make that tea, Daphne.

(*There is a slight pause.*

DAPHNE *looks helplessly at Shirley, then at the bouquet, crosses and exits* R)

(*She sits on the edge of the settee at the right end*) It's no use talking like that, Shirley, and it's no use trying to fool yourself. If you waited from now till Doomsday, he wouldn't turn up. As far as marrying your precious Albert Tufnell goes, you've 'ad it.

(SHIRLEY *sobs*)

(*She painfully removes her shoes and rubs her feet*) "Waited a bit longer"! I thought I'd die of shame as it was. Everybody whispering and sniggering . . .

SHIRLEY. Don't, Mum!

EMMA (*as she eases a foot out of a shoe*) Ooooh! That's better. (*She returns to the subject in hand*) And poor Mr Purefoy——

SHIRLEY. I'll never be able to face the Vicar again.

EMMA. —standing there trying to pretend he wasn't there at all. (*She puts on her slippers*)

SHIRLEY (*suddenly sitting up*) But, Mum—(*almost wildly*) what am I going to *do*? Won't I ever see Albert again?

EMMA (*removing her hat*) You'll see him again, my girl, if there's any justice at all in this world. But you won't see him in church. Where you'll see him is in the Police Court. (*She stabs her hat with the hatpin*)

SHIRLEY (*almost howling*) Oh, no, Mum! No, not that. I couldn't bear it.

EMMA. You don't think he's going to be let get away with this, do you?

SHIRLEY. But, Mum, I couldn't. (*She sobs*) Oooh, it's all dreadful! I don't know what I'm going to do. I'll never live it down. (*Now bordering on hysteria*) Albert, where are you? I want you. I want you.

EMMA. Shirley, dear, don't talk about him, love. Don't think about him.

SHIRLEY. What's the use of saying that? How can I help thinking about him? I love him. Oooh! (*She bursts into a flood of tears*)

(EMMA *rises with her shoes and hat and moves up* C)

EMMA. He'll pay for this. You see if he doesn't—I always said he was no good, didn't I?

SHIRLEY. Stop it, Mum! Stop running him down. I can't bear it. Oh, I wish I could die. Oh, Albert, where are you?

EMMA. I'll tell you where he probably is at this very . . .

HENRY. Let up on the girl, Emma. What's the use of carrying on at her? You're only making things worse than they are already.

EMMA (*moving to* L *of Henry; flaring*) How you have the nerve to so much as open your mouth after what you've done . . .

HENRY. Me? What have I done?

EMMA. What have you . . .! You've ruined your daughter's life, that's all.

HENRY (*roused*) What the hell are you talking about?

EMMA. Who brought Albert Tufnell to this house in the first place? You did. (*She puts her shoes on the floor* R *of the sideboard*)

HENRY. But, dammit, I didn't tell Shirley to go and fall in love with him, did I?

EMMA. If she'd never 'ave seen 'im, she *wouldn't* 'ave, would she?

HENRY (*wearily*) For Gawd's sake . . .

EMMA (*with fine scorn*) You and your poor sailor boy that you met at the *White Hart*—your poor sailor boy with no friends—and wanted a bed for the night. "Must be kind to our Jolly Jack Tars", you said. Well, where's your Jolly Jack Tar *now*? I expect he's being jollier than ever—somewhere the other side of England. (*She puts her hat on the sideboard*)

SHIRLEY (*with a loud sob*) Carnoustie? Mum, I must talk to Carnoustie.

EMMA (*moving above the settee; with grander scorn*) Carnoustie! There's another of 'em. Let him dare to set foot in this house . . .

SHIRLEY. But, Mum, I *must* see him. Mum, where is he?

EMMA (*scornfully*) Looking for Albert. But he knows as well as I do that he has as much chance of finding him as a needle in a haystack.

(DAPHNE *enters* L. *She carries a tray of tea-things*)

I wouldn't be surprised if Carnoustie didn't know all along what Albert was going to do. (*She moves to the window and stands with her back to the audience*)

DAPHNE (*putting the tray on the table*) I'm sure you're wrong there, Aunt Emma.

(EMMA *turns*)

It's hard enough to believe there's any wickedness in Albert, but I'm *sure* there's none in Carnoustie. If he'd known, he would never have let Shirley be humiliated like this.

EMMA. Oh, my Lord! Don't tell me that *you've* fallen for a sailor, now?

DAPHNE. I'm just telling you what I think, that's all. The tea won't be a minute. The kettle's boiling.

(DAPHNE *exits* R)

HENRY (*unfortunately*) And I could do with a cup.

EMMA (*rounding on Henry*) You could do with a cup of tea—you don't suppose you're going to just sit sipping tea, do you? That's right! Take your boots off! Take your collar off. (*She moves to* L *of Henry*) And your tie. In fact, if I were you, I should pop upstairs and nip into bed and have a little nap for a couple of hours. I shouldn't let the fact that my daughter's been jilted *and* it's my fault—I shouldn't let that bother you too much. (*With a change of tone, low and almost menacing*) 'Enry 'Ornett, you'll put on your

boots, your collar and tie again right away and get yourself down
to the police station and tell 'em they've got to find Albert
Tufnell if they search all England to do it.

SHIRLEY (crying) No, Mum. I won't let you do that! The
p-p-police c-c-can't make him m-m-marry me if he doesn't
want to.

EMMA. It's no use talking that way. 'Enry! Are you going or
aren't you?

HENRY. I aren't.

EMMA. What!

HENRY. You 'eard. This is Shirley's concern, not yours. An'
if she doesn't want to do nothing about it . . .

EMMA (moving to the sideboard) Very well, then—then I'll go
myself.

SHIRLEY. Mother, if you do, I'll—I'll drown myself, I swear
I will.

(DAPHNE enters R. She carries a pot of tea which she puts on the tray)

EMMA (moving to R of the table; baffled) Oh, well, 'ave a cup of
tea, then perhaps you'll see sense.

DAPHNE (up L of the table) Aunt Emma, I just saw Mrs Lack
coming through the . . .

(MRS LACK's voice, appropriately solemn, is heard off R)

MRS LACK (off) Are you there, Emma?

EMMA (under her breath) Now if she starts . . . (She sits R of the
table. To Daphne) Give Shirley a cup of tea.

(DAPHNE pours one cup of tea.
  MRS LACK enters R)

MRS LACK. It's all right, Emma. It's only me. I wouldn't have
intruded at a time like this, but I thought I'd just . . . (She crosses
to R of the settee) Shirley love, my 'eart goes out to you.

SHIRLEY. I—I . . .

EMMA. Florrie, I'm sure you mean this very kindly, but . . .

MRS LACK. I'm not going to stay. (She sits R of Shirley on the
settee) I know you want to be alone with your great sorrow, but
I just felt I had to . . .

(DAPHNE hands the cup of tea for Shirley over the back of the settee)

(She automatically takes the cup) Oh, thank you, love. (She sips the tea)

(DAPHNE pours three cups of tea, hands one to Emma, one to
Henry, then sits L of the table)

Oh, I needed that. I went to Banfields with all the others, Emma,
same as you told us, but could I eat a bite! Not if you'd paid me
a thousand pounds. My 'eart was with poor Shirley 'ere. So I
said to myself, "Florrie, it's no use. Your place isn't here. Where

you should be is near those who are suffering"—and, Gawd, '*ow* you must be suffering!

(HENRY *sits morose and glum*)

EMMA. It's very kind of you, Florrie, but . . .

MRS LACK (*to Henry*) Mr 'Ornett—poor Mr 'Ornett—you're not saying much, are you? But if we could look into your 'eart, I'm sure we'd find it filled with a black 'atred for the man who's treated your flesh and blood so shamefully.

HENRY (*with meaning*) You'd find it filled with black hatred for *somebody*.

MRS LACK (*sailing on*) But why should it 'appen to poor Shirley, here, that's what I keep asking myself. Why? (*With a big heave of the shoulders*) Ah, well! "The Lord moves in a mysterious way His wonders to perform." Did he leave a note or anything?

EMMA (*shortly*) Who? The Lord?

MRS LACK. No. The bridegroom.

SHIRLEY (*sitting upright*) Oooh! I never thought of that. Mum, Daphne, can you see a note anywhere?

EMMA. You'll find no notes—believe me.

MRS LACK (*heavily*) Perhaps he's thrown himself in the river, sooner than face . . . (*She looks at Emma*)

EMMA (*sharply*) Face what?

MRS LACK. His responsibilities.

EMMA (*rising*) I'm facing one very big fact at the moment, and that is . . .

(CARNOUSTIE *enters* L)

Oh! It's you.

SHIRLEY (*rising and running to Carnoustie*) Carnoustie—have you found him—have you heard anything?

CARNOUSTIE (*dejectedly shaking his head*) No, I've no'.

SHIRLEY. Have you looked—everywhere?

CARNOUSTIE. Aye, I ha'e.

SHIRLEY. Oh, Albert! (*She weeps*)

CARNOUSTIE. I'm awfu' sorry. I've done ma best.

EMMA (*moving above the table*) You're sorry! Well, that's something, I must say.

DAPHNE. Aunt Emma, please . . .

EMMA (*brushing her aside with a gesture*) I just want to ask you one question, young man. Did you know about it? Did Albert tell you he was going to do this?

CARNOUSTIE. No. He did not.

HENRY. 'Course he didn't.

EMMA (*to Henry*) Quiet, you! (*To Carnoustie*) Do you know *why* he did it?

CARNOUSTIE (*hedging*) I think Shirley would be more likely to know that than me.

EMMA. You *do* know, don't you?

CARNOUSTIE. I know no more than you know yourselves.

EMMA (*moving down* RC) It wouldn't surprise me if you'd put him up to it—right from the start.

DAPHNE. That's not fair, Aunt Emma. Why should Carnoustie do that? And why should he know the reason any more than you —if as much?

EMMA (*moving to* R *of the table*) And what do you mean by that, Daphne Pink? I don't know that way of talking. If you've got something to say, say it. Don't go throwing out a lot of nasty incinuendos. And as for you, young man, you can be thinking of getting yourself away from here. (*She moves down* R)

(*The front door is heard to open and close with a slam*)

Now who . . .?

(MRS LACK *rises and moves above the table, and puts her cup on it.* DAPHNE *rises and moves above the settee*)

SHIRLEY (*clutching Daphne*) Oh, Daphne, suppose it's Albert.

(EDIE *enters quickly* L. *She is wild-eyed and almost hysterical. She stands inside the doorway for a moment, panting, then moves to* L *of the table*)

Aunt Edie! (*She moves down* LC)

DAPHNE. Auntie . . .

(EDIE *cannot speak, but, with a howl, which increases in volume as she moves, comes down to Shirley and flings herself at her, round her and over her. She pushes Shirley on to the settee.* DAPHNE *closes the door* L. MRS LACK *moves to* R *of the table.* CARNOUSTIE *is behind the left end of the settee*)

SHIRLEY (*before she goes under*) Aunt Edie!

(EDIE *hugs Shirley, kisses her and almost smothers her*)

EMMA (*sharply, but unavailingly*) Now then, Edie, none of that!

(EDIE *continues to hug Shirley*)

Edie. Do you hear me?

MRS LACK. You'll 'ave to do *something*, Emma.

(EMMA *crosses to Edie and tries to pull her away from Shirley*)

EMMA. Stop it, d'y'hear! (*In a fury*) Edie 'Ornett, will you . . . (*She struggles to pull Edie away*) Do you want to—smother her? (*She drags Edie below the table*) Haven't you a grain of sense?

EDIE (*hysterically*) It's happened again! It's happened to poor Shirley—same as it happened to me. I knew it. I *knew* it! Ooooooh! (*She breaks loose from Emma and flings herself on Shirley, sitting* R *of her on the settee*)

Mrs Lack. Oooh! Isn't she awful!

Emma. Henry, she's your sister. Can't *you* stop her?

Edie. I saw it! I saw it in the tea-cup! (*She looks wildly around*) You saw it, too, didn't you, Mrs Lack?

Mrs Lack. Well—I . . .

Edie. A bleeding, broken heart. Oh, my poor lamb! (*She flings herself on Shirley*)

Emma. Will you shut up and leave Shirley alone! (*She drags Edie behind the table and stands between her and the settee*)

Edie. Ever since I saw it in the tea-cup I've known. Wherever I've turned I've seen bleedin' broken hearts—and they were *all* Shirley's—I knew they were Shirley's. Something told me.

Emma (*shouting*) Will you be quiet a minute while *I* tell you something.

Edie (*ignoring Emma*) Another Great Sorrow in the family. Oh, my poor Shirley. I know—I *know* what you're going through —I've suffered it, too. The shame! The humiliation!

Shirley (*by now almost in Edie's condition*) Don't, Aunt Edie! Don't!

(Daphne *moves below the left end of the settee and comforts Shirley*)

Edie. But that it should happen to you—same as it's happened to me—left at the altar rails . . .

Shirley. Oooh!

Emma (*almost dancing with fury*) Edie 'Ornett!

Edie. That's twice in the family. Twice it's 'appened. It's a curse. That's what it is. It's a *curse*!

Mrs Lack (*horrified*) What!

Emma. Will you . . .!

Edie (*with every ounce of drama she can put into it*) A curse on the 'ouse of 'Ornett! (*She collapses on the chair above the table and weeps*)

Mrs Lack. The Lord save us!

Shirley (*weeping*) Aunt Edie!

Carnoustie (*clearing his throat uncomfortably and moving to the door* l) Well, I think it's time I was going—if you'll excuse me.

Emma. We will.

Daphne (*moving between Carnoustie and the door* l) If you'll wait a minute while I change, Carnoustie, I'll walk down to the station with you.

Carnoustie. Och—well, all right.

Emma. Well, of course, you must please yourself, but I *do* think, *and* I shall certainly tell your mother when I write, that you're behaving proper 'eartless, Daphne Pink.

Daphne. But why—what have I done?

Emma. Does it mean nothing to you that your own cousin has been deceived and made a fool of?

Daphne (*baffled*) Of course it does. I'm as sorry for poor Shirley as any of you.

EMMA. But it doesn't stop you throwing yourself at the best friend of the man who did it—does it?

DAPHNE. Aunt Emma, you can't blame Carnoustie for what Albert has done.

EDIE (*with great daring*) And you can't even blame poor Albert.

EMMA (*turning on Edie*) I thought I told you to be quiet.

EDIE (*rising*) Albert's not to blame. It's Fate! That's what it is. And Fate used Albert for its tool.

MRS LACK (*to Emma*) Oh, Lord! She's off again.

EDIE. "The moving finger writes and having *wrote*, moves on."

EMMA (*now livid*) I've had all I'm going to stand of it. (*She crosses to L of Henry*) Listen to me, 'Enry 'Ornett. I've put up with this crackpot of a sister of yours——

(EDIE *whimpers and sits above the table.* DAPHNE *rushes to L of Edie and puts her arms around her*)

| SHIRLEY DAPHNE EMMA | (*together*) | Mother! Oh, poor Aunt Edie! Don't listen. —for the past twenty years. God knows how I've done it, but I have. But I've finished—do you hear? I'm through! I've had all I can stand of her "Fates", her "tea-cups", her Great Sorrows and bleedin' hearts, and I tell you, here and now, that *she* leaves this house to-morrow morning. And if *she* doesn't, then I *do*! |

(HENRY *reacts*)

SHIRLEY. Mum, you can't turn poor Aunt Edie out like that. It isn't fair. She's upset, that's all.

EMMA (*rounding on Shirley*) Now don't you start telling me what I *ought* to do. I should think you've got enough on your plate, without bothering your head about anyone else. (*She crosses to R of the settee*) You 'aven't managed your *own* affairs so marvellously, yourself, 'ave you? Gettin' yourself tied up with a good-for-nothing fly-by-night from God knows where, and making yourself and all your family fools of in front of the whole town.

(*There is an outburst of protestations from everyone.* SHIRLEY *and* EDIE *weep.* MRS LACK *moves to L of Henry*)

| DAPHNE SHIRLEY HENRY CARNOUSTIE MRS LACK | (*together*) | Aunt Emma. Oh, Mum, you don't realize what you're saying. Now then, Missus! Mrs Hornett, for shame on ye! Far be it from me . . . |

(*All the above can be added to, ad lib. While the hubbub is at its height, the door* R *opens.* ALBERT *enters* R. MRS LACK *moves behind the armchair.* HENRY *rises. There is complete and utter silence for a very long time as they realize Albert is standing there*)

ALBERT (*presently; very simply*) 'Ullo.

(*There is a long pause, then* SHIRLEY *rises, runs to Albert and flings her arms around him*)

SHIRLEY. Albert! Oh, Albert! (*She sobs wildly*)

(ALBERT *makes as if to put his arms around Shirley, but stops himself. The hubbub breaks out again*)

CARNOUSTIE		⎧Albert! Man! Where have you been?
EMMA		⎪So you've turned up, have you? Well,
	(*together*) ⎬	let me tell you . . .
DAPHNE		⎪Oh, thank God! Thank God!
MRS LACK		⎩Well, far be it from me . . .

(*All the above can be added to ad lib.*)

SHIRLEY (*when the hubbub has ceased*) Oh, Albert, where have you been?

(ALBERT *appears to be overwhelmed by all the enquiring looks*)

ALBERT. I—I . . .
SHIRLEY (*desperately*) Albert, where *have* you been?
ALBERT. I've been looking at Pop's ferrets.

(EMMA, *almost tearing her hair out, moves down* L *and stands with her back turned to the rest of the family*)

SHIRLEY (*staggered*) You've been . . .?

(*The others make inarticulate noises of surprise*)

Albert Tufnell, are you completely *mad*?
ALBERT (*quietly*) No, I'm not. At least, I hope I'm not.
SHIRLEY. But—but . . . (*words fail her*)
EMMA (*turning*) Well, I've *tried* to keep quiet—I have tried . . .
ALBERT (*quietly*) Try a bit harder, Ma.
EMMA. What!
HENRY (*sitting in the armchair*) He said, "Try a bit harder."
SHIRLEY. But don't you realize what you've done? Our wedding . . .
MRS LACK. What happened? (*Almost hopefully*) Did you lose your memory, or something?
ALBERT. No, I didn't lose my memory.
SHIRLEY. Then—are you telling me that you did what you did, deliberately?

ALBERT. Yes, I am.

SHIRLEY. You let me go to church, *knowing* that you weren't going, too?

ALBERT. Yes, I did.

SHIRLEY (*desperately*) Oh, Albert, I couldn't have believed that —that anyone could have done such a cruel thing, but, Albert, that doesn't matter. Nothing matters if only you'll tell me you *still* love me and want to marry me.

ALBERT. I love you, Shirl—just as I've always done—and I still want to marry you.

SHIRLEY (*brokenly*) Oh, thank God! Thank God!

EMMA. I can't stand it. Watching my own daughter cheapening herself, begging and pleading with a man to marry her. (*She sits on the settee at the left end*)

SHIRLEY (*wildly*) I don't care, Mum. (*She weeps*) I don't care if I am cheapening myself. All that I know is that I want Albert to marry me and he's going to.

ALBERT. I didn't say I was.

SHIRLEY. What?

ALBERT. I said I *wanted* to—not that I was going to.

SHIRLEY (*bewildered*) But, Albert . . .

ALBERT (*moving down* R) It isn't always best to do the things we want.

SHIRLEY (*with a step towards Albert*) I—I don't understand you, Albert. You're just standing there, talking in riddles—and if it's any satisfaction to you to know it, you're breaking my heart.

EDIE (*rising and moving to Shirley*) Shirley, my poor, poor, Shirley.

SHIRLEY (*putting her arms around Edie and sobbing on her shoulder*) Oh, Aunt Edie . . .

ALBERT (*to Emma*) You've never wanted me to marry Shirl, have you, Ma?

EMMA. I never *have*—and you've done nothing today to make me change my mind.

ALBERT. I've always known you didn't. God knows, you've made it plain enough.

EMMA. And I'll tell you something else. I'd rather give her to the first man who comes through that door—even if it was the devil himself.

(*The* REVEREND OLIVER PUREFOY *enters* L. *He is aged about forty. He has an easy manner, a pleasant voice and is a likeable person, not given to throwing his weight about, but quite capable of using it, and with authority, when needed*)

PUREFOY (*as he enters; gently*) May I come in? (*He stands up* L)

(*There is a gasp from* EMMA, *then a truly ghastly pause*)

(*Aware of their gaping*) The front door was unlocked, so I took the liberty . . .

(HENRY *rises*)

EDIE		Emma, it's the Vicar. It's Mr Purefoy.
SHIRLEY	*(together)*	Oh, Mr Purefoy!
EMMA		Oh!
MRS LACK		Oh, well, *now*, of course . . .
CARNOUSTIE		(*To Albert*) You're for it the noo.

(HENRY *resumes his seat*)

EMMA (*faintly*) Come in, Mr Purefoy.

PUREFOY (*moving to* R *of the settee*) Thank you, Mrs Hornett.

SHIRLEY (*moving to Albert and leading him forward a step*) Mr Purefoy, this is . . .

PUREFOY (*waving his hand*) No, please. Don't let us bother with formal introductions; at a time like this, I'm sure you're all far too disturbed. (*He looks around*) Actually, I think I saw you all in church, did I not?

EMMA (*pointing to Albert*) Not *him*, you didn't.

PUREFOY. Oh, perhaps I . . .

SHIRLEY. Mr Purefoy, this—this is Albert.

PUREFOY (*not understanding*) Albert? (*He moves below the table*)

(ALBERT *crosses to* R *of Purefoy and shakes hands with him*)

How do you do—er—Albert? (*With a start*) Good heavens! You mean—*Albert*—er—*the* Albert?

SHIRLEY (*vigorously nodding her head*) Ummps!

PUREFOY (*nonplussed*) Oh—well—I—the missing bridegroom, eh?

EMMA		Missing bridegroom. If you ask me, there's more missing than . . .
MRS LACK		He's turned up, sir. Better late than never.
SHIRLEY	*(together)*	But, Mr Purefoy, he says he doesn't want to . . .
ALBERT		I'm sorry I've caused all this trouble, sir . . .

SHIRLEY (*clearly*) He says he loves me, but he won't marry me.

PUREFOY (*waving his hand*) Forgive me, I . . . (*He silences them*) I am a little confused. Perhaps if—er—*one* person could explain . . .?

EMMA. *I'll* soon do that.

(ALBERT *moves down* R)

PUREFOY (*a little dejectedly perhaps*) Oh! I did think perhaps . . . (*He waves towards Shirley and Albert*) However . . . (*He takes a step towards Emma and prepares to listen*) Yes, Mrs Hornett?

EMMA. Well . . .

CARNOUSTIE (*piping up*)   If there's any explanation to be made, sir, I should think Albert's the one to do it.

PUREFOY (*heartily*)   So should I.

EMMA.   Very well, Mr Purefoy. *Let* him explain, then, but don't believe one word he says.

MRS LACK.   I know if my daughter was ever treated the way poor Shirley's been . . .

EDIE.   I *still* say, and I'll go on saying it, that Albert's not to blame. It's Fate, and it's no use fighting *Fate*, is it, Mr Purefoy?

PUREFOY.   Er—Fate, Miss Hornett?

EDIE.   I saw it in the tea-cup, sir.

EMMA (*to Edie*)   I thought I told you . . .

PUREFOY.   Please! (*With a suggestion of authority in his voice*) I came here to offer what comfort I could to—er—Shirley.

EMMA.   And it was very kind of you, Mr Purefoy . . .

PUREFOY (*taking Emma down; firmly*)   After all, I baptized her, and I prepared her for Confirmation, and I still hope it will be my privilege to marry her.

EMMA.   But not to him.

PUREFOY (*over-riding her; more firmly*)   As I say, I came to offer comfort, but it would appear that I might be able to offer something more concrete—er—given the opportunity. I should like to have a word with—(*he waves a hand towards Shirley and Albert*) these two young people. (*He moves to R of Emma*) Don't you think it would be wiser if those who are not primarily concerned were to leave us for a while, Mrs Hornett?

DAPHNE (*immediately*)   Come on, Carnoustie. (*She moves to the door* L)

EMMA.   Well, I don't see what good . . . Very well. (*Sharply*) Henry—off you go.

(MRS LACK *hopefully sits tight*)

HENRY (*rising; to Emma*)   But aren't *you* . . .?

EMMA (*to Mrs Lack; sharply*)   And you, Florrie.

MRS LACK (*moving reluctantly to the door* R)   Well, I should have thought I *was* concerned, seeing Rita was going to be a bridesmaid.

(MRS LACK *exits* R.
    EDIE *exits up* R.
    HENRY *rises and follows her off*)

CARNOUSTIE (*moving above the table*)   Albert.

ALBERT.   What?

CARNOUSTIE.   If you need me—call out.

(DAPHNE *and* CARNOUSTIE *exit* L)

PUREFOY (*with a bland smile*)   I'm afraid I'm treating your house as though it were my own, Mrs Hornett—driving *you all* out like this.

(EMMA *sniffs*)

But I'm sure that a word or two with these children—alone . . .

EMMA. Very well, Mr Purefoy—I don't see what good can come of it. The sooner it's all over, and *him* out of the house, the better.

PUREFOY. But . . .

EMMA. But as you wish, Mr Purefoy. *As* you wish.

PUREFOY. Thank you. (*He pauses*) I did—er—(*with a step towards Emma*) suggest "alone", Mrs Hornett.

EMMA (*after looking around*) Well, we *are* alone.

PUREFOY (*after coughing discreetly*) I—er—meant . . .

EMMA (*aghast*) You mean "alone" without *me*. Is that what you mean?

PUREFOY (*gently*) I'm afraid it is.

EMMA. As Shirley's mother I've a right to be here.

PUREFOY. Only if each of these two wants you to be.

SHIRLEY. You'd better go, Mum.

PUREFOY. Is that your wish, too, Albert?

ALBERT. If Shirl and me can't hear what you've got to say, sir, without her mother being here—then we might as well chuck in our hands straight away.

PUREFOY (*coughing discreetly*) H'm!

EMMA (*rising*) Well, if I go, I go under protest.

PUREFOY. Er—quite. Very natural—perhaps. (*He moves to the door* L *and opens it*)

EMMA (*moving up* L) And, if you don't mind my saying so, Mr Purefoy, I don't know why you want *Shirley* here. (*She points to Albert*) He's the one that's done wrong—not her. My girl gave a promise to him and was prepared to keep it—but not his lordship here. Oh, no. He let her down. He's made her look like a fool in front of the whole town. And not satisfied with that, he has the nerve to come back here just so we can see him gloating over the misery he's caused.

ALBERT (*quietly*) Are you going, Ma—under protest?

EMMA (*snapping at him*) Yes, I am. (*To Shirley*) And I'm expecting you to come with me.

SHIRLEY. No, Mum, I'm staying.

EMMA. You'll regret it—you see if you don't—as sure as your name is Shirley 'Ornett.

PUREFOY (*with an easy smile*) But I'm hoping we may yet change it to Shirley *Tufnell*.

EMMA. Oooh!

(EMMA *exits angrily* L. *There is silence for a moment.* PUREFOY *closes the door*)

PUREFOY (*breaking the silence*) Ahem! A—woman of character, Mrs Hornett.

(ALBERT *gives Purefoy a look*)

(*He catches the look on Albert's face and coughs*) Well—now. Let us sit down, shall we? (*He moves down* c *and sits on the downstage edge of the table*)

(SHIRLEY *sits on the settee.* ALBERT *is about to sit beside her.* SHIRLEY *looks reproachfully at* ALBERT, *and he sits* L *of the table*)

Now, Albert—you said, a moment ago, something about— Shirley and you hearing what *I've* got to say.

ALBERT. Yes, sir.

PUREFOY. But you're quite wrong there, you know. It isn't what *I* have to say that matters.

ALBERT. Oh?

PUREFOY. Good heavens! Surely you must see that *some* explanation of your extraordinary—and that's putting it mildly, Albert—your extraordinary behaviour is expected?

ALBERT (*muttering*) Yessir.

PUREFOY. Do you still love Shirley?

ALBERT. Yessir.

PUREFOY (*rising and moving to* R *of Shirley*) And, Shirley, you love Albert?

SHIRLEY. He knows I do.

PUREFOY. Then—Albert—Shirley—where the devil have we come unstuck? (*He pauses*) Albert, I think this is where you begin to talk. (*He crosses above the table and pats Albert's shoulder*) Now, come along. (*He pauses*) If it helps you at all to know this, I'm convinced that, in spite of the callous, the cruel thing you have done to Shirley this morning, basically you're—all right.

ALBERT. Thank you, sir.

PUREFOY. Of course, I may be wrong; first impressions, you know. But I am waiting for you to *prove* that I am right.

ALBERT. I didn't turn up at church this morning because— well, for one thing, I was frightened.

PUREFOY. Frightened? Of what?

ALBERT. The future—mine and Shirley's.

PUREFOY (*incredulously*) You . . .?

ALBERT. I mean—whether we'd be able to make a go of it— or whether *I* would, I should say.

PUREFOY (*sharply*) My dear Albert, that's nonsense. (*He turns on Albert with something of a Prosecuting Counsel's manner*) You seriously ask us to believe that you gave no thought to the future, and your ability to cope with it, until this morning—a few hours before your wedding?

ALBERT (*wretchedly*) I thought about it all last night. I never slept a wink.

(PUREFOY *moves* R *of the table and leans over it. One almost hears the swish of the gown as he moves*)

PUREFOY. For heaven's sake! Man—last night was a hundred years too late to start thinking. You should have thought about it, *and* arrived at a definite conclusion long ago.

ALBERT (*trying to fight back*) How could I, when it didn't happen until last night.

PUREFOY. When *what* didn't happen?

ALBERT (*lamely*) Er—what *happened*.

PUREFOY (*moving down* R) Albert—at this moment I am sorely tempted to kick you hard in the pants.

SHIRLEY (*protesting*) Oh, no, Mr Purefoy, you mustn't . . .

PUREFOY (*with a grand gesture of hopelessness; patiently*) Shirley, you don't seem to understand. (*He points at her*) You are on my— (*he points to himself*) side. If I can't get him to talk sense, then I am damn well going to kick it out of him.

SHIRLEY. If Albert doesn't want to marry me, sir, I wouldn't want you to force him to—not in any way.

ALBERT. I *do* want to—you know I do.

PUREFOY (*vigorously*) Then why don't you? (*He moves to the chair* R *of the table and sits*)

(*There is a long pause.* ALBERT *nervously twiddles his fingers*)

ALBERT (*presently*) I don't know whether you know it or not, sir, but I was brought up in an Orphanage. So—I've never had any—real—"home life". Whenever I've had a leave I've always stayed at the—Y.M.C.A.s—the Union Jack Club or the Salvation Army—you know, sir. (*He rises and moves down* R) Well, when I was "on board" I used to hear other lads talking about—their homes; their mums; their dads—their families—and it sort—of made me "homesick" for—for the home I'd never had—if you follow me, sir. And I made up my mind that when the right girl came along I was going to *have* a home of my own, even if it was only a couple of rooms to start with. I've only had two long leaves since I got to know Shirl and both times I've—stayed here. (*He pauses*) I've had my first taste of "home life", sir, and—(*to Shirley*) you're not going to like this very much, Shirl—(*to Purefoy*) but if what I've seen in this house is "honest-to-God home life", then all I can say is, give me the Salvation Army.

SHIRLEY (*weeping quietly*) Albert!

(*There is a pause*)

PUREFOY (*embarrassed*) Albert, I can't believe you're justified in thinking the way you do, but let me assure you that if, or when, you marry and settle down in a home of your own, that home will be just as happy as you and your wife *make* it.

ALBERT (*after a look at Shirley; quietly*) As we're *allowed* to make it.

PUREFOY. I don't follow you.

ALBERT (*with a step towards Purefoy*) I thought that once we had a place of our own—me and Shirl—we'd be O.K. We'd have our ups and downs, naturally, and I don't suppose we would always see eye to eye—but at least we'd be *on* our *own* and we'd sort things out ourselves and in our own way.

PUREFOY. And that's how it *will* be. Why not? You're going to work in Badcaster when you leave the Navy, aren't you?

ALBERT. Yes, sir.

PUREFOY. Well, there you are. If you marry Shirley, I presume you will find some place, even if it is, as you say it might be, only a couple of rooms.

ALBERT. That would do me.

PUREFOY. I started my married life in *one*. In the luxury of your *two* rooms, Albert, you will lay the foundations of your future happiness.

(*There is a pause.* ALBERT *looks directly at Shirley*)

ALBERT (*crossing to* R *of Shirley*) Will we, Shirl?

(SHIRLEY *covers her face with her hands and sobs bitterly*)

PUREFOY (*surprised*) Shirley! What is it? Don't you want that?

SHIRLEY (*from behind her hands*) Yes—yes.

PUREFOY. Then why in heaven's name . . .?

(*There is a pause*)

ALBERT (*quietly*) I *know*, Shirl—about the house. (*He pauses*) You know that, don't you?

SHIRLEY (*after a pause; very quietly*) Yes, Albert.

PUREFOY. You know—what? Is there something you two haven't told me? (*He moves below the table. After a pause*) Something that justifies your conduct this morning, Albert?

ALBERT (*moving to* L *of Purefoy*) I don't know about that, sir. But I think it explains it.

SHIRLEY (*brokenly*) It *does* justify it, Albert. I see that now. I've seen it all along, really.

PUREFOY (*moving between Albert and Shirley*) Then why have you allowed me to cluck away like a broody hen when all the time . . .? (*Impatiently*) What is this whatever it is, for goodness' sake?

(ALBERT *looks at Shirley*)

SHIRLEY (*after a pause*) I—I've played a dirty trick on Albert, Mr Purefoy.

(PUREFOY *looks first at Shirley, then at Albert*)

PUREFOY. Oh?

SHIRLEY. Yes, sir. I—I let mum put down the deposit on a

house—to buy it, I mean—for Albert and me. I never said anything to Albert about it. I wasn't going to tell him; not until we
were married.

PUREFOY. But why not?

SHIRLEY. Because I knew he'd never agree to it.

PUREFOY. But, surely . . .

SHIRLEY. You see, sir—the house is only three doors away from
this one—Number Twenty-Four.

PUREFOY (*very gravely*) Oh! (*He crosses below Albert and stands
down* R)

SHIRLEY. I can't think why I let mother do it.

PUREFOY. Without consulting Albert—it was very wrong of
you, Shirley. (*To Albert*) And that is why you've missed the boat,
so to speak?

ALBERT (*moving to* L *of Purefoy*) Yes, sir. I wouldn't have known
if Aunt Edie hadn't let it slip out last night. I felt I was being—
tricked into something, and what sort of a way is that to start
your married life, sir? Well, all last night I lay awake thinking
about it. And I thought to myself, "Suppose we do come to live
at Number Twenty-Four—what will the result be?" And no
matter which way I looked at it, I knew it wouldn't work. (*He
pauses and moves* RC) I don't know what I've done to make her
hate me as she does . . .

PUREFOY (*quietly*) Done to whom, Albert?

ALBERT (*after a slight pause*) Mrs 'Ornett, sir. Shirley's mum.
She *does* hate me, she's let me see that she does. Don't ask me
why. I've done everything I can to get her to think differently,
but no matter what I do only seems to make things worse. I say
to myself, "She hates *you*, Albert, but she doesn't seem to like
anybody *else* very much, either." (*He moves to* R *of the table*) The
way she treats Pop and poor Aunt Edie—it makes me run hot
and cold—and the thought of her living three doors away running
in and out of *my* home—filling it with hatred . . . (*His voice rises*)
No! (*He sits* R *of the table and covers his face with his hands for a
moment*) My God, no!

(PUREFOY, *after a pause, moves to* R *of Albert and pats him com-
fortingly on the back*)

Well, now you know, sir, why I didn't show up at my wedding
—what with the trick over the house and knowing what would
happen if we moved in at Number Twenty-Four.

PUREFOY (*moving above the table; quietly*) What you did was the
wrong thing, but I can almost understand why you didn't do the
right one.

ALBERT. Thank you, sir; and I'm sorry, Shirl, that I've had to
speak of your mum the way I have.

(SHIRLEY *turns her head away.*

HENRY *pokes his head round the door* R, *then comes quietly into the room and listens*)

PUREFOY. Albert, there's one thing you haven't explained. Why did you come back—here—now?

ALBERT. To ask Shirley to marry me, sir.

PUREFOY (*staggered*) To *what?*

ALBERT. On my terms, I mean. I made up my mind last night that I'd got to be firm, so I decided I'd skip the wedding and come back here, and if Shirley saw things as I see them, and if she loved me enough—well, we'd get married just as soon as we could.

HENRY (*moving down* R) Yes, and if only I'd had the courage to do the same . . .!

SHIRLEY (*seeing Henry*) Dad!

HENRY. If you've half the sense I think you have, my girl, you'll go down on your knees and beg Albert to marry you, and then you'll tell your mother just what she can do with Number Twenty-Four.

SHIRLEY. But, Dad, she's put a deposit on the house.

HENRY. And she can do the same with the deposit. (*He moves to* R *of Purefoy*) Mr Purefoy, I don't want you to think that I'm being—disrespectful about my wife.

PUREFOY (*blankly*) Aren't you?

HENRY. No, sir.

PUREFOY. Good heavens!

HENRY. But I understand 'er. Albert doesn't; there's no reason why he should, but understanding 'er wouldn't put things right as far as 'e's concerned.

PUREFOY. If only Mrs Hornett could learn to like Albert . . .

HENRY. What good would that do? It wouldn't stop 'er trying to make 'is life a misery.

PUREFOY. But, Mr Hornett . . .

HENRY (*moving down* R; *almost desperately*) She can't *help* it, sir. It's just *her*, and why should Albert stand for it? With me, it's different. I'm her husband, and besides she's done a lot that I have to be thankful for.

ALBERT (*incredulously*) You have, Pop?

HENRY. Yes, Albert, I have. (*He pauses briefly*) Take a look round this room. Nothing sort of wonderful, you might say, but it's a home I'd never be ashamed for anyone to see. *She* keeps it this way. If you went into some of the 'ouses in this street . . . And another thing, I've never yet come 'ome from work and found Emma at the pictures and a packet of fish and chips waiting for me in the oven. And that's a damn sight more than most husbands in my position can say.

PUREFOY (*moving to* L *of the table*) That is *very* true.

HENRY. And she's been—sort of ambitious. Not for 'erself—

that's the funny part of it. You'd think with Emma it *would* be, but no—first for me—and then when I didn't turn out much of a success—for Shirley here. And you don't suppose it's been much fun for her saddled with Edie all these years. It isn't every wife that would have stood for that, you know.

PUREFOY (*moving down* L *of the table*) You're very proud of Mrs Hornett, aren't you?

HENRY (*simply*) Aye, I am. And I'm fond of her. There are times when I could wring her blasted neck if I had the courage . . .

PUREFOY. Ahem!

HENRY (*moving to* R *of Purefoy*) But, Mr Purefoy, I'm speaking as man to man, now. I *am* fond of her, and I believe she's fond of me, but it doesn't stop her trying to make me miserable. It's a kink she's got. I can put up with it, but what I'm trying to say is, that there's no reason why Albert should.

PUREFOY. Then what you suggest is . . .

(EMMA *is suddenly heard sobbing loudly outside the door* L)

(*He looks towards the door* L) Good heavens! Who is . . .?

ALBERT (*overlapping*) What the . . .! (*He rises*)

HENRY (*in a voice of panic*) It's 'er. Has she been listening?

SHIRLEY (*rising and running to the door* L) Mum!

HENRY (*yelling*) My Gawd! Let me get out of here while I'm still alive.

(HENRY *dashes off* R)

SHIRLEY (*opening the door* L) Mum!

(EMMA *enters* L *and stands just inside the door. She is weeping noisily.* SHIRLEY *moves above the settee*)

PUREFOY. Mrs Hornett!

SHIRLEY (*amazed*) Mum, what is it?

ALBERT (*shattered*) Well, stone a crow!

(EMMA *moves to the settee and sits.* PUREFOY *stands* R *of the settee*)

EMMA (*wretchedly*) Don't talk to me. I couldn't stand it. I've been listening. I've heard every word that's been said. They say listeners never hear any good of themselves—and I've been punished.

ALBERT. Good Lord!

EMMA. I'm a wicked woman, Mr Purefoy.

PUREFOY (*bending over Emma; soothingly*) No, no, Mrs Hornett.

EMMA. I am. I must be. All the misery I've caused. Making Henry's life a hell on earth. But I didn't do it with wicked intent, Mr Purefoy, I swear I didn't.

PUREFOY. No, I'm sure you didn't, Mrs Hornett.

EMMA. And hearing Henry stick up for me like that. That man's a jewel, Mr Purefoy.

(PUREFOY *and* ALBERT *look at each other*)

And I'm an evil woman. Mr Purefoy, what can I do to be saved?

PUREFOY (*blinking*) I *beg* your pardon?

EMMA (*with just a trace of bite in her voice*) Well, you're a clergyman; you should know.

PUREFOY (*not happy*) Mrs Hornett, I—this is so sudden. (*He realizes what he has said*) Ahem!

EMMA (*weeping*) I didn't know—I didn't realize I was making everyone miserable. I—I—just thought I was—just looking after their interests. (*She finishes in a wail*)

PUREFOY. Yes, yes, you meant well, Mrs Hornett, I'm quite sure of that. But you were—misguided in your method of approach, shall we say?

EMMA (*obligingly*) Yes, *let's* say that. You see, Mr Purefoy, I've always had to manage other people 'cos they've never been able to manage themselves.

PUREFOY. Did you give them the chance to?

EMMA. No. There wasn't any point; you see, Henry—doesn't know what he's doing half the time, and Edie—well, she doesn't know what she's doing *any* of the time; so you see . . .

PUREFOY. And Shirley? What about Shirley?

EMMA. Whatever I've done for Shirley, I've done with the best intentions. (*She weeps, reaches over the back of the settee and takes Shirley's hand*)

(SHIRLEY *moves below the settee*)

I have, Shirley, love, I *have*.

SHIRLEY. I'm sure you have, Mum.

EMMA. That's why I put the deposit down on Number Twenty-Four. I thought it would be nice for you to have me near you, a sort of guardian angel. (*To Purefoy*) You see, Mr Purefoy, sir, I knew he was a sailor, and—well, you know what sailors are.

PUREFOY. I know what *this* one is, Mrs Hornett. He's a grand fellow who will make Shirley a good husband, and who will make you proud to have him for a son-in-law.

EMMA (*humbly*) If *you* say so, Mr Purefoy.

PUREFOY (*to Albert*) I can only say that I wish he were *my* son-in-law.

EMMA (*between sobs; reflectively*) Yes, *your* daughter hasn't made a very good catch for herself, has she?

PUREFOY (*moving up* L; *between annoyance and embarrassment*) I— I . . .

EMMA (*nearly in tears*) Dear, oh, dear! There I go again. Saying things that aren't nice. Oooh! Making people miserable. Do you think I'm too old to reform, Mr Purefoy?

PUREFOY (*moving to* L *of the table*) If I may be forgiven a platitude . . .

(EMMA *speaks from now on in almost humble acquiescence, broken by an occasional return to her old style and self*)

EMMA. Yes, sir? I'm sure we'll *all* forgive you.

PUREFOY. I was merely going to say, "It's never too late to mend."

EMMA (*weeping*) Where's Henry? (*Like a small child*) I want Henry.

(SHIRLEY *crosses above the settee to the door* R)

ALBERT (*moving to the fireplace; muttering*) My Gawd! She wants Henry.

SHIRLEY (*opening the door* R *and calling*) Is dad there, Aunt Edie? (*She moves above the table*)

(EDIE *enters* R *and moves to* R *of the table*)

EDIE (*as she enters*) He's out with his ferrets. (*She sees the weeping Emma*) Why, Emma . . .!

EMMA (*with all the old bite*) Tell him if he doesn't leave them blessed ferrets . . . (*She realizes she is speaking sharply*) Oooh! (*She gulps*) Ask him if he'll come in, will you, Edie?

EDIE (*surprised*) Ask him?

EMMA. Yes, *please.*

(EDIE *gropes for the door* R, *finds it, and totters through it*)

ALBERT. Don't overdo it, Ma. Think of our weak 'earts.

EMMA (*sobbing*) I—I don't know what I'm going to do.

PUREFOY. Then I'll tell you, if I may?

EMMA. Do, Mr Purefoy, please.

PUREFOY. You are going to dry your tears; collect all your friends and relations; and bring them all down to St Michael's in half an hour.

EMMA. What—what for?

PUREFOY. For the wedding of your daughter Shirley to Albert Tufnell, A.B.

SHIRLEY (*wildly*) Mr Purefoy! You mean that?

PUREFOY. Certainly, if Albert does.

ALBERT (*excitedly*) Can you *do* that, sir?

PUREFOY. Of course. Why not?

EMMA (*weeping*) Oooh!

ALBERT. What about it, Shirl?

SHIRLEY (*running to Albert*) Oh, Albert, darling.

(ALBERT *and* SHIRLEY *embrace, then she moves to the mirror*)

PUREFOY. Shall we say in half an hour?

ALBERT (*moving to* R *of Purefoy*) Thank you, sir. (*He holds out his hand*) And thank you, sir. (*He shakes hands with Purefoy*)

PUREFOY. My dear boy, for what?

ALBERT (*lowering his voice*) For being so understanding about ma and me.

PUREFOY (*lowering his voice still further*) My dear Albert— (*almost guiltily*) I was speaking with the voice of sad experience. You see, I—I happen to have a mother-in-law myself. (*He picks up his hat and moves to* L *of the table*) In half an hour then, Mrs Hornett.

(EMMA *takes her compact from her handbag and powders her nose.* PUREFOY *nods with a melancholy grimace.* ALBERT *follows suit.*

PUREFOY *exits* L)

SHIRLEY (*in a panic of joy*) Half an hour! I'll never be ready. Oh! Where's Daphne? (*She runs to the door* L) Where's my bridesmaid?

ALBERT. With my best man, I expect.

EMMA. We'll have to hurry. Where's Henry?

SHIRLEY (*calling*) Daph-ne! (*She opens the door*) Oh!

(CARNOUSTIE *and* DAPHNE *almost fall into the room as they break from an embrace.* CARNOUSTIE'S *mouth is liberally adorned with lipstick*)

Oh!

DAPHNE. *Oh!*

CARNOUSTIE. Och—I . . . Och!

(EMMA *rises and crosses down* R)

ALBERT. Dinna stand there "Och-ing" ·

(CARNOUSTIE *gives a guilty start, and fumbles wildly for his handkerchief*)

And away out and fetch those taxis back. I'm getting married in half an hour.

CARNOUSTIE. Wha'! *Again?*

(SHIRLEY *crosses to* L *of Albert*)

ALBERT. I am so.

DAPHNE (*moving to Shirley and hugging her*) Oh, Shirley! How wonderful.

ALBERT (*to Carnoustie*) What are we waiting for? I'm getting married, do you hear?

CARNOUSTIE. Aye, I heard. Man, I've an awfu' fear that ma feet are on the same dread, slippery slope as your ain.

(CARNOUSTIE *exits* L)

EMMA (*moving to the sideboard*) Now come along, Shirley. (*She*

picks up the bridal veil and coatee and hands them to Shirley) It's time
you were seeing about getting yourself made presentable. Go
upstairs; and, Daphne, you go with her. Give your face a good
wash.

DAPHNE. Why? Have I smeared my lipstick?

EMMA. I was talking to Shirley.

(DAPHNE *exits* L. SHIRLEY *runs to the mirror* R, *fiddles with her
veil, then crosses towards the door* L)

SHIRLEY. Oh, my veil.

ALBERT (*intercepting Shirley*) Come here, Shirl.

SHIRLEY. Yes, Albert?

ALBERT. You're sure you *want* to marry me?

SHIRLEY. Oh, Albert! (*She embraces him*)

(HENRY *enters* R)

HENRY (*as he enters*) Edie says you want me.

EMMA (*bustling*) Yes, I do. You're to go upstairs right away,
give yourself a wash, brush your coat, and get yourself ready for
the wedding.

HENRY (*blinking*) What! *Another* wedding?

EMMA (*sharply*) No; the same one. Go on. Off you go. Do as
I tell you.

(HENRY *crosses towards the door* L)

Henry! Come back.

(HENRY *stops, turns and moves to* L *of Emma*)

(*She plants a smacking kiss on Henry's cheek*) There!

(*The others react*)

HENRY (*when he has partly recovered*) 'Ave you been drinking?

(HENRY *staggers off* L)

EMMA (*to Albert*) I've started it. (*With a sudden start*) Oh, my
Lord! I've just remembered. (*She goes to the door* R *and calls*) E-die!

(EDIE *enters* R. *She carries a pot of tea*)

EDIE. Yes, Emma? I was just making a cup of tea. I thought
you needed it.

EMMA. Never mind about the tea. Go down to *Banfields* right
away and tell everybody they've got to stop eating.

EDIE. What!

EMMA. They're to go straight back to the church at once—the
wedding's in half an hour.

EDIE (*in ecstasy*) No! Oh, Emma . . . !

EMMA. Go on. Hurry!

EDIE (*moving towards the door* R) I'll just get my hat . . .

EMMA (*pushing Edie towards the door* L; *firmly*) You'll get down there right away. There won't be a thing left if you don't. Lord! I 'ope they 'aven't started on the wedding cake. (*She stands* R *of the sideboard and puts on her shoes*)

(EDIE *plants the teapot on the left side of the sideboard and runs to Shirley*)

EDIE. Oh, I'm so happy for you. (*She kisses Shirley, then moves to Albert*) Oh, Albert!

ALBERT (*hugging Edie*) I ought to be marrying you, really.

EDIE (*moving to the sideboard*) Oh, Albert. (*She sees the teapot on the sideboard, stops dead and looks at it in terror*) Oooh!

EMMA. What . . .? (*She sees the teapot and hastily picks it up*) You . . .! (*She holds the teapot for a split second and gulps*) Never mind, love.

EDIE. *What!*

EMMA. I said, "never mind". (*She puts the teapot firmly on the table*)

EDIE. She's going mad.

(EDIE *exits* L. EMMA *moves to* L *of Albert*)

EMMA. Well, Albert, I don't know whether it's for the best or not, but—(*she kisses him*) I'm sure I *hope* you'll be happy.

(ALBERT *puts his right arm around Shirley, and his left arm around Emma*)

ALBERT. We will. Don't worry. (*Very confidentially*) But I'll tell you *one* thing—Ma.

EMMA. What's that—son?

ALBERT (*confidentially whispering to her out of the corner of his mouth*) We're not going to live at Number Twenty-*bloody*-Four.

CURTAIN

FURNITURE AND PROPERTY LIST

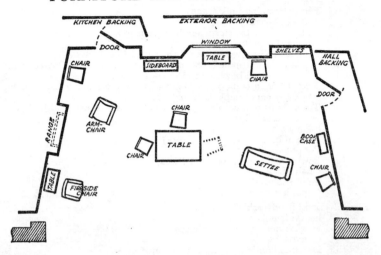

ACT I

On stage—Put-U-Up settee. *On it:* cushions
       Dining-table. *On it:* cloth
       5 upright chairs
       Armchair. *On it:* cushion, chair-back
       Fireside chair (down R)
       Table (down R). *On it:* radio
       Sideboard. *On it:* ornaments, crumb-tray and brush
               In drawer: tablecloth, clothes brush
               In cupboard: handbag with usual contents
       Table (under window). *On it:* vase of flowers
       Shelves (up L). *On them:* gong, cruet set, set of table mats, etc.
       Wall cabinet (L). *On it:* books
       Kitchen range. *On it:* saucepan
       Fire-irons
       Club fender
       Hearth rug
       On mantelpiece: clock, ornaments, scissors, pins, letters, greeting cards
       In hearth: Henry's slippers
       Pictures on walls
       Window curtains
       Carpet on floor
       Coat hooks (L of door up R)
       Electric pendant
       Mirror (down R)
       Light switch (below door R)

Curtains open
Fire lit
Light off

Off stage—Teapot with tea (EDIE)
        Cardboard box. *In it:* wedding cake (EDIE)
        Tray. *On it:* 2 cups, 2 saucers, 2 teaspoons, jug of milk, basin of
            sugar, slop basin (EDIE)
        Tin of furniture polish and duster (EDIE)
        Cup, saucer, teaspoon (EMMA)
        Pan of steaming milk (EDIE)
        Kitbag (ALBERT)
        Suitcase. *In it:* towel, sponge bag (ALBERT)
        Kitbag (CARNOUSTIE)
        Suitcase. *In it:* towel, sponge bag, parcel (CARNOUSTIE)
        Suitcase. *In it:* undies, panties, nightdress, brassiere, parcel with
            rose bowl, wrapped bottle of scent (DAPHNE)
        Tray. *On it:* 7 cups, 7 saucers, 7 teaspoons, 2 mats, 7 small plates,
            7 paper napkins (EDIE)
        Tray. *On it:* 7 large plates, jug of milk, basin of sugar, dish of jam,
            cruet (EMMA)
        7 knives, 7 forks (EDIE)
        Plate of bread and butter (EMMA)
        Pot of tea (EMMA)
        Bowl of salad, plate of meat (EDIE)
        Chair (EMMA)
        Stool (EDIE)
        Jug of hot water (EDIE)

Personal—EDIE: handkerchief
        EMMA: handkerchief
        HENRY: pipe, pouch of tobacco
        CARNOUSTIE: half a crown
        DAPHNE: handbag. *In it:* ladder stop
        ALBERT: handkerchief, packet of cigarettes

ACT II

SCENE 1

Strike—Everything from table C
        Wedding cake
        Rose bowl
        Sailor caps
        Stool
        1 chair
        Move 1 chair from L of the table to L

Set—Tea-chest (down L). *In it:* brown paper for filling
        Newspapers for wrapping (down L)
        Ornaments for packing (on table C)
        Chair above the table.

Close curtains
Light on
Fire lit

Off stage—Tray. *On it:* table mat, 4 cups, 4 saucers, 4 teaspoons, jug of milk,
            basin of sugar (DAPHNE)
        Pot of tea (EDIE)
        Cup, saucer and spoon (EDIE)
        2 sheets, eiderdown, blanket (EMMA)
        2 pillows (SHIRLEY)
        2 pillows (EDIE)

Personal—ALBERT: cigarettes, matches, handkerchief.

SCENE 2

Strike—Bedclothes
       Clothing
       Kitbags
       Cases
       Broken ornaments
       Albert's cap

Set—*On back of armchair:* Henry's jacket
      Move chair above table to L

Tidy room
Re-set chairs
Close bed
Open curtains
Fire on
Light off

Off stage—Handbag (EMMA)
         Cellophane bag. *In it:* bridal bouquet, 2 bridesmaids' posies, 3 car-
                nation buttonholes (EMMA)
         Dead ferret (HENRY)

Personal—CARNOUSTIE: comb, wedding ring
         MRS LACK: handbag. *In it:* powder compact
         ALBERT: cigarettes, matches

ACT III

Set—*In cupboard up* L: Emma's slippers
    In fireplace: Henry's slippers
    Chair from L above table

Curtains open
Fire lit
Light off

Off stage—Tray. *On it:* 4 cups, 4 saucers, 4 teaspoons, jug of milk, basin of
               sugar (DAPHNE)
         Pot of tea (DAPHNE)
         Pot of tea (EDIE)

Personal—EMMA: handbag. *In it:* compact

Any character costumes or wigs needed in the performance of this play can be hired from Charles H. Fox Ltd, 184 High Holborn London W C 1

LIGHTING PLOT

Property Fittings Required—electric pendant c, fire grate (both practical)

Interior. A living-room. The same scene throughout

THE APPARENT SOURCES OF LIGHT ARE—in daytime: a window back LC, and at night: an electric pendant c

THE MAIN ACTING AREAS ARE—at the fireplace R, at a sideboard up C, at a table C and at a settee LC

ACT I   A September afternoon

To open: Effect of afternoon daylight outside window
  Fire, on
  Pendant, off
  Strips outside doors R and L, on

No cues

ACT II   SCENE 1   Evening

To open: Blue outside window
  Fire, on
  Pendant, on
  Strips outside doors R and L, on

No cues

ACT II   SCENE 2   Morning

To open: Lighting as Act I

No cues

ACT III   Morning

To open: Lighting as previous scene

No cues

MADE AND PRINTED IN GREAT BRITAIN BY
BUTLER & TANNER LTD, FROME AND LONDON

MADE IN ENGLAND

52   34   89

PHILIP KING & FALKLAND CARY

"SAILOR, BEWARE!"

GB 573 01395 0

35p
net

7s
net